G000252314

GCSE
Success

AQA

Physics

Revision
Guide

Complete
Revision & Practice

Dan
Foulder

Contents

Forces

Forces

Scalar quantities have magnitude only.

Vector quantities have magnitude and an associated direction.

A vector quantity can be represented by an arrow. The length of the arrow represents the magnitude, and the direction of the arrow represents the direction of the vector quantity.

At **terminal velocity** the downwards force on the skydiver (weight) is equal to the upwards force (air resistance). As these forces have the same magnitude, the vector arrows representing them are the same length.

600N

600N

Contact and non-contact forces

A force is a push or pull that acts on an object due to the interaction with another object. Force is a vector quantity. All forces between objects are either:

➤ contact forces – the objects are physically touching, for example:
  friction, air resistance, tension and normal contact force
  or
➤ non-contact forces – the objects are physically separated, for example:
  gravitational force, electrostatic force and magnetic force.

Gravity

➤ **Weight** is the force acting on an object due to gravity.
➤ All matter has a gravitational field that causes attraction. The field strength is much greater for massive objects.
➤ The force of gravity close to the Earth is due to the gravitational field around the Earth.
➤ The weight of an object depends on the gravitational field strength at the point where the object is.
➤ The weight of an object and the mass of an object are directly proportional (weight $\propto$ mass). Weight is a vector quantity as it has a magnitude and a direction. Mass is a scalar quantity as it only has a magnitude.
➤ The weight of an object can be thought of acting on a single point called the 'centre of mass'.

Weight is measured using a calibrated spring-balance – a **newtonmeter**.

Weight can be calculated using the following equation:

> **weight = mass × gravitational field strength**
> $$W = mg$$
> ➤ weight, W, in newtons, N
> ➤ mass, m, in kilograms, kg
> ➤ gravitational field strength, g, in newtons per kilogram, N/kg

Example:
What is the weight of an object with a mass of 54 kg in a gravitational field strength of 10 N/kg?

weight = mass × gravitational field strength
= 54 kg × 10 N/kg
= 540 N

Air resistance

Friction

Resultant forces

The resultant force equals the total effect of all the different forces acting on an object. In the skydiver example on the opposite page the resultant force on the skydiver is 0 as the downward force is equal to the upwards force.'

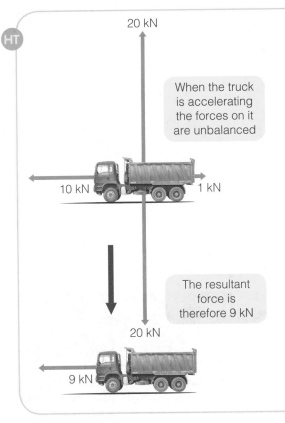

20 kN

When the truck is accelerating the forces on it are unbalanced

10 kN   1 kN

The resultant force is therefore 9 kN

20 kN

9 kN

If the forces on an object are balanced, the resultant force is zero. If the object is stationary it remains stationary and if it is moving it continues moving at a constant speed.

A single force can be resolved into two components acting at right angles to each other. The two component forces together have the same effect as the single force.

Work done and energy transfer

Work is done when a force causes an object to move. The force causes a displacement.

The work done by a force on an object can be calculated using the following equation:

> **work done = force × distance moved along the line of action of the force**
>
> $$W = Fs$$
>
> ➤ work done, W, in joules, J
> ➤ force, F, in newtons, N
> ➤ distance, s, in metres, m (s represents displacement, commonly called distance)

Draw two more large diagrams of the truck shown at the top of the page. Alter the force arrows to represent the truck decelerating and the truck stationary.

Example:

What work is done when a force of 90 N moves an object 14 m?

work done = force × distance moved along the line of action of the force

work done = 90 × 14 = 1260 J

One joule of work is done when a force of one newton causes a displacement of one metre.

1 joule = 1 newton metre

Work done against the frictional forces acting on an object causes a rise in the temperature of the object.

1. What is the difference between a vector quantity and a scalar quantity?
2. Give two examples of contact forces.
3. What is the weight of a 67 g object in a gravitational field strength of 10 N/kg?
4. What is 78 Nm in joules?

Forces and elasticity

Inelastically deformed

Elastically deformed

When an object is stretched and returns to its original length after the force is removed, it is **elastically deformed**.

When an object does not return to its original length after the force has been removed, it is **inelastically deformed**. This is **plastic deformation**.

Extension

The extension of an elastic object, such as a spring, is directly proportional to the force applied (extension ∝ force applied), if the limit of proportionality is not exceeded.

➤ **Stretching** – when a spring is stretched, the force pulling it exceeds the force of the spring.
➤ **Bending** – when a shelf bends under the weight of too many books, the downward force is from the weight of the books, and the shelf is resisting this weight.
➤ **Compressing** – when a car goes over a bump in the road, the force upwards is opposed by the springs in the car's suspension.

In order for any of these processes to occur, there must be more than one force applied to the object to bring about the change.

The force on a spring can be calculated using the following equation:

> force = spring constant × extension
> $F = ke$
> ➤ force, F, in newtons, N
> ➤ spring constant, k, in newtons per metre, N/m
> ➤ extension, e, in metres, m

Example:
A spring with spring constant 35 N/m is extended by 0.3 m. What is the force on the spring?

$F = ke$
$= 35 \times 0.3$
$= 10.5$ N

This relationship also applies to the compression of an elastic object, where the extension e would be the compression of the object.

A force that stretches (or compresses) a spring does **work** and **elastic potential energy** is stored in the spring. Provided the spring does not go past the limit of proportionality, the work done on the spring equals the stored elastic potential energy.

Spring balance

Force and extension

Force and extension have a linear relationship.

If force and extension are plotted on a graph, the points can be connected with a straight line (see Graph 1).

The points in a non-linear relationship cannot be connected by a straight line (see Graph 2).

Graph 1 – Linear relationship

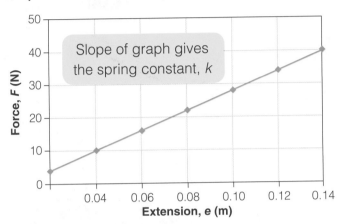

Slope of graph gives the spring constant, k

Graph 2 – Non-linear relationship

In order to calculate the spring constant in Graph 1, take two points and apply the equation.

So, spring constant $= \dfrac{\text{force}}{\text{extension}}$

$= \dfrac{10}{0.04}$

$= 250 \text{ N/m}$

Attach a number of objects of different masses to an elastic band and measure how far the band extends. Repeat the investigation again using an plastic bag instead of a rubber band. How do your results compare?

1. What is the force of a spring with an extension of 0.1 m and a spring constant of 2 N/m?
2. When is the extension of an elastic object, such as a spring, directly proportional to the force applied?
3. What type of energy is stored in a spring?

Moments, levers and gears

Levers

Moments

The turning effect of a force is called the **moment** of the force.

The moment of a force is given by the following equation:

> moment of a force = force × distance to pivot
>
> $$M = Fd$$
>
> ➤ moment of a force, M, in newton metres, Nm
> ➤ force, F, in newtons, N
> ➤ distance to pivot, d, is the perpendicular distance from the pivot to the line of action of the force, in metres, m

> **Example:**
> A 30 cm spanner is used with a force of 36 N. What is the moment?
>
> $M = Fd$
> $\quad = 36 \times 0.3$
> $\quad = 10.8$ Nm

If an object is balanced, the total clockwise moment about a pivot equals the total anticlockwise moment about that pivot.

> the sum of clockwise moments = the sum of anticlockwise moments

For example:

1.5 m

3 m

10 N

Moment = 10 × 3
= 30 N/m

Pivot

20 N

Moment = 20 × 1.5
= 30 N/m

Levers

A lever reduces the force needed to carry out an action. The force is exerted around a pivot.

Levers and gear systems can both be used to transmit the rotational effects of forces. Levers and gears act as force multipliers, exerting a larger force than is being exerted on them.

For example:

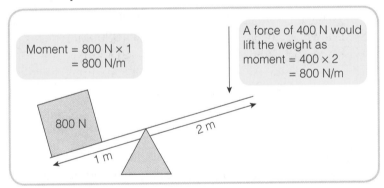

Moment = 800 N × 1
= 800 N/m

A force of 400 N would lift the weight as moment = 400 × 2
= 800 N/m

800 N

1 m

2 m

A **gear system** can also be used to transfer the rotational effect of forces. The teeth of gears interlock so when the first gear in a system rotates, it rotates the other gears that it is interlocked with. Two interconnected gears will rotate in opposite directions.

If gears are different sizes, the smaller gear in a system will rotate faster than the larger gear.

Input

Output

Close a door by pushing it at 10 cm intervals from the edge of the door towards the hinge. What do you notice about the force required as you move from the edge of the door towards the hinge?

1. What is a moment?
2. What statement can be made about the moments on a balanced object?
3. What is the moment when a force of 72 N is applied with a 0.7 cm lever?

Pressure in a fluid

Fluids

Liquids and gases are **fluids**.

The pressure in a fluid is caused by the fluid and the surrounding atmospheric pressure. The pressure causes a force to act at right angles (normal) to a surface. The pressure exerted on a surface by a fluid can be calculated using the following equation:

$$\text{pressure} = \frac{\text{force normal to a surface}}{\text{area of that surface}}$$

$$p = \frac{F}{A}$$

➤ pressure, p, in pascals, Pa
➤ force, F, in newtons, N
➤ area, A, in metres squared, m^2

Example:
What is the pressure of a force of 650 N over an area of 0.50 m^2?

$$\text{pressure} = \frac{\text{force normal to a surface}}{\text{area of that surface}}$$

$$= \frac{650}{0.5}$$

$$= 1300 \text{ Pa}$$

HT The pressure exerted by a column of liquid can be calculated using the following equation:

$$\text{pressure} = \frac{\text{height of}}{\text{the column}} \times \frac{\text{density of}}{\text{the liquid}} \times \frac{\text{gravitational}}{\text{field strength}}$$

$$p = h\rho g$$

➤ pressure, p, in pascals, Pa
➤ height of the column, h, in metres, m
➤ density, ρ, in kilograms per metre cubed, kg/m^3
➤ gravitational field strength, g, in newtons per kilogram, N/kg

Example:
What is the pressure at a depth of 40 m in seawater? (density of seawater = 1029 kg/m^3 and gravitational field strength = 10 N/kg)

$$\text{pressure} = 40 \times 1029 \times 10$$

$$= 411.6 \text{ kPa}$$

Pressure increases in a column of liquid as there are more particles applying the pressure. If the height of the column increases or the density of the liquid increases, this causes an increase in the number of particles and so increases the pressure.

HT Upthrust

A partially or totally submerged object experiences a greater pressure on the bottom surface than on the top surface. This creates a resultant force upwards. This is **upthrust**.

An object less dense than the surrounding liquid displaces a volume of liquid equal to its own weight. This object floats as its weight is equal to the upthrust.

An object more dense than the surrounding liquid is unable to displace a volume of liquid equal to its own weight. This object sinks as its weight is greater than the upthrust.

The boat floats as weight and upthrust are equal

The anchor sinks as its weight is greater than the upthrust

Atmospheric pressure

The atmosphere is a thin layer (relative to the size of the Earth) of air round the Earth. The atmosphere gets less dense with increasing altitude. The air molecules colliding with a surface create atmospheric pressure.

As height of an object increases, there are fewer air molecules above the object so their total weight is smaller. This means that as height increases, atmospheric pressure decreases.

Carry out an investigation using a pin. First, place the pin onto some water in a glass and observe what happens. Then, put the pin on top of a small piece of paper and place the paper and pin onto the water. Observe the results.

HT **1.** What is the pressure in a 13 m column of water? (density of water = 1000 kg/m³ and gravitational field strength = 10 N/kg)

HT **2.** Explain, in terms of forces, why an object sinks.

3. Why does air pressure decrease with height?

Speed and velocity

5

Distance and speed

Distance is how far an object moves. As distance does not involve direction, it is a scalar quantity.

Displacement includes both the distance an object moves, measured in a straight line from the start point to the finish point, and the direction of that straight line. As displacement has magnitude and a direction, it is a vector quantity.

The speed of a moving object is rarely constant. When people walk, run or travel in a car, their speed is constantly changing.

The speed that a person can walk, run or cycle depends on:

Some typical speeds are:
- walking – 1.5 m/s
- running – 3 m/s
- cycling – 6 m/s
- car – 20 m/s
- train – 35 m/s

The speed of sound and the speed of wind also vary.

A typical value for the speed of sound in air is 330 m/s. A gale force wind is one with a speed above 14 m/s.

For an object travelling at a constant speed, distance travelled can be calculated by the following equation:

> **distance travelled = speed × time**
> $$s = vt$$
> ➤ distance, *s*, in metres, m
> ➤ speed, *v*, in metres per second, m/s
> ➤ time, *t*, in seconds, s

Example:
What distance is covered by a runner with a speed of 3 m/s in 6000 seconds?

$$
\begin{aligned}
\text{distance travelled} &= \text{speed} \times \text{time} \\
&= 3 \times 6000 \\
&= 18\,000 \text{ m} \\
&= 1.8 \text{ km}
\end{aligned}
$$

Velocity

The **velocity** of an object is its speed in a given direction.

As velocity has a magnitude and a direction, it is a vector quantity.

Keywords

Displacement ➤ Distance travelled in a given direction

Velocity ➤ Speed in a given direction

HT A car travelling at a constant speed around a bend would have a varying velocity because it is changing direction.

When an object moves in a circle, the direction of the object is continually changing. This means that an object moving in a circle at constant speed, such as an orbiting satellite, has a continually changing velocity.

Time how long it takes to travel to school. Use a mapping website to calculate the distance. Now calculate the average speed of your journey. Replicate this investigation on different days. Is there much variation in your average speed?

1. Why is distance a scalar quantity?
2. What is the speed of a walker who covers 10 km in 2.5 hours?
3. What is the difference between speed and velocity?

Distance–time and velocity–time graphs

6

Keyword
Acceleration ➤ Change in velocity over time

Distance and time

The distance an object moves in a straight line can be represented by a distance–time graph.

The speed of an object can be calculated from the gradient of its distance–time graph.

The graph below shows a person jogging.

Distance–time graph

The average speed of this jogger between 0–120 seconds can be worked out as follows:

$$\text{speed} = \frac{\text{distance}}{\text{time}} = \frac{400}{120} = 3.33 \text{ m/s}$$

The speed of an accelerating object can be determined by using a tangent to measure the gradient of the distance–time graph.

Acceleration

Acceleration can be calculated using the following equation:

$$\text{average acceleration} = \frac{\text{change in velocity}}{\text{time taken}}$$

$$\left[a = \frac{\Delta v}{t} \right]$$

➤ acceleration, a, in metres per second squared, m/s^2
➤ change in velocity, Δv, in metres per second, m/s
➤ time, t, in seconds, s

Example:
A car travels from 0 to 27 m/s in 3.8 seconds. What is its acceleration?

$$\text{change in velocity} = 27 - 0 = 27 \text{ m/s}$$
$$\text{average acceleration} = \frac{\text{change in velocity}}{\text{time taken}}$$
$$= \frac{27}{3.8} = 7.1 \text{ m/s}^2$$

An object that slows down (decelerates) has a negative acceleration.

The acceleration of a runner who goes from 0 m/s to 3 m/s in 5 seconds is $\frac{(3-0)}{5} = 0.6$ m/s^2

Measure out a short distance and roll a ball. Time how long it takes the ball to travel the distance you've measured. Plot the distance travelled and the time taken on a graph. Repeat the investigation, but this time roll the ball harder. Again, plot the result on the same speed-time graph. Compare the gradients of the two lines. What do you notice? Use your graph to calculate the average speed of the two balls.

Velocity–time graph

Acceleration can be calculated from the gradient of a velocity–time graph.

 Distance travelled can be calculated from the area under a velocity–time graph.

The graph below shows the movement of a car.

Velocity–time graph

The acceleration between 0–50 seconds can be worked out as follows:

$$\text{gradient of line} = \frac{\text{velocity}}{\text{time}}$$

$$= \frac{20}{50} = 0.4 \text{ m/s}^2$$

As the gradient of the line is steeper between 200–250 seconds than it is between 0–50 seconds, the acceleration must have been greater between 200–250 seconds.

 The distance travelled between 0–200 seconds can be worked out as follows:

Area from 0–50s $= \left(20 \times \dfrac{50}{2}\right) = 500$ m

Area from 50–200s $= 20 \times 150 = 3000$ m

Total distance travelled $= 3500$ m

The equation below applies to uniform motion:

final velocity^2 – initial velocity^2 = 2 × acceleration × distance

$$v^2 - u^2 = 2\,as$$

➤ final velocity, v, in metres per second, m/s
➤ initial velocity, u, in metres per second, m/s
➤ acceleration, a, in metres per second squared, m/s^2
➤ distance, s, in metres, m

Falling objects

Near the Earth's surface, any object falling freely under gravity has an acceleration of about 9.8 m/s^2. This is the gravitational field strength, or acceleration due to gravity, and is used to calculate weight.

An object falling through a fluid initially accelerates due to the force of gravity. Eventually the resultant force will be zero and the object will move at its terminal velocity.

The terminal velocity graph shows the speed of a skydiver over time.

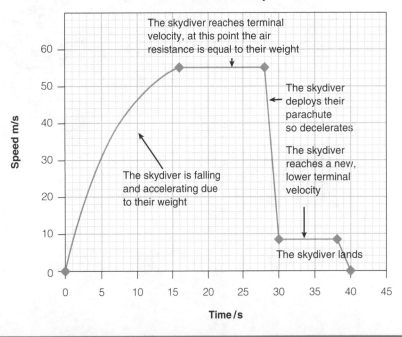

Terminal velocity

The skydiver reaches terminal velocity, at this point the air resistance is equal to their weight

The skydiver deploys their parachute so decelerates

The skydiver reaches a new, lower terminal velocity

The skydiver is falling and accelerating due to their weight

The skydiver lands

1. What does the gradient of a distance–time graph represent?
2. What type of acceleration will an object which is slowing down have?
 3. What does the area under a velocity–time graph represent?

Mind map

Contact vs non-contact

Spring constant

Scalar vs vector

Work done and energy transfer

Elastic deformation

Forces

Elasticity

Resultant forces

FORCES

Inelastic deformation

Displacement

Pressure in a fluid

Velocity

Distance

Atmospheric pressure

Upthrust

Acceleration

Speed

Practice questions

1. a) The gravitational field strength on Mars is 3.7 N/kg.

    What would be the weight of a Mars rover with a mass of 187 kg?   **(2 marks)**

    b) Would the weight of the rover be different on Earth?
    Explain your answer.   **(2 marks)**

    c) A water container on Mars has a height of 3 m. Water has a density of 1000 kg/m³.

    What is the pressure at the bottom of the container?   **(2 marks)**

2. The graph below shows the velocity of an object.

    a) Use the graph to calculate the:

    i)   acceleration from 0–3 seconds.   **(2 marks)**

    ii) distance travelled in 3 seconds.   **(2 marks)**

    b) Was the acceleration between 0–3 seconds greater than the acceleration
    between 3–6 seconds?
    Explain your answer.   **(2 marks)**

7

Newton's laws

Newton's first law

Newton's first law deals with the effect of resultant forces.

➤ If the resultant force acting on an object is zero and the object is stationary, the object remains stationary.

➤ If the resultant force acting on an object is zero and the object is moving, the object continues to move at the same speed and in the same direction (its velocity will stay the same).

➤ When a vehicle travels at a steady (constant) speed the resistive forces balance the driving force.

Stationary object – zero resultant force

Object moving at constant speed – zero resultant force

Newton's first law means that the velocity of an object will only change if a resultant force is acting on the object.

Examples of resultant force:

A car is stationary. At this point the resultant force is zero.

The car starts to move and accelerates. As it is accelerating, the resultant force on the car is no longer zero.

The car travels at a constant velocity. The resultant force is zero again.

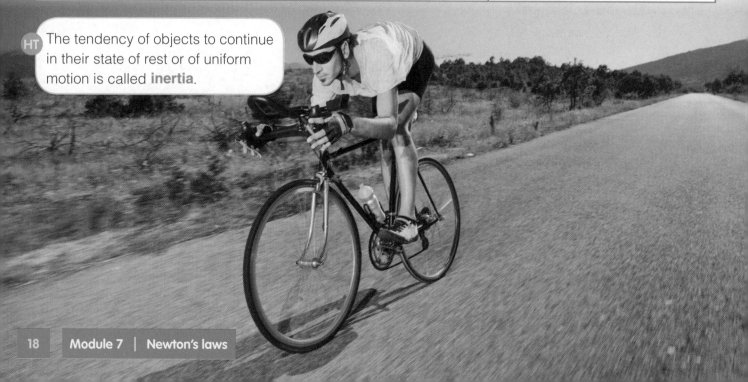

HT The tendency of objects to continue in their state of rest or of uniform motion is called **inertia**.

Newton's second law

The acceleration of an object is proportional to the resultant force acting on the object, and inversely proportional to the mass of the object.

Therefore:

> acceleration $\propto$ resultant force
>
> resultant force = mass × acceleration
> - force, F, in newtons, N
> - mass, m, in kilograms, kg
> - acceleration, a, in metres per second squared, m/s²

Newton's third law

Whenever two objects interact, the forces they exert on each other are equal and opposite.

When a fish swims it exerts a force on the water, pushing it backwards. The water exerts an equal and opposite force on the fish, pushing it forwards.

Example:
A motorbike and rider of mass 270 kg accelerate at 6.7 m/s². What is the resultant force on the motorbike?

$$270 \times 6.7 = 1809 \text{ N}$$

If the motorbike maintains a constant speed (e.g. 27 m/s) the resultant force would now be 0 (as acceleration = 0, $270 \times 0 = 0$).

HT **Inertial mass** is a measure of how difficult it is to change the velocity of an object. It is defined by the ratio of force over acceleration.

Make a revision poster with a drawing illustrating each of Newton's laws and the resultant force equation.

1. A book of weight 67 N is on a desk. What force is the desk exerting on the book?
2. A sprinter of mass 89 kg accelerates at 10 m/s². What is the resultant force?
3. What happens to the speed of a moving object that has a resultant force of 0 acting on it?

Forces and braking

Stopping distance

The stopping distance of a vehicle is a sum of the **thinking distance** and the **braking distance**.

stopping distance = thinking distance (the reaction time of the driver) + braking distance (distance the vehicle travels under the braking force)

A greater vehicle speed leads to a greater stopping distance (given a set braking force). As the vehicle is going faster, the car will travel further in the time taken for the driver to react and apply the brakes.

As the mass of a vehicle increases the braking distance also increases. Thinking distance remains the same. This means that a bus would have a longer braking distance than a car and therefore a longer stopping distance.

The graph below shows the stopping distances over a range of speeds for a car.

Typical stopping distances

Speed	Thinking distance	Braking distance	Total
20 mph (32 km/h)	6 m	6 m	12 metres, 3 car lengths
30 mph (48 km/h)	9 m	14 m	23 metres, 6 car lengths
40 mph (64 km/h)	12 m	24 m	36 metres, 9 car lengths
50 mph (80 km/h)	15 m	38 m	53 metres, 13 car lengths
60 mph (96 km/h)	18 m	55 m	73 metres, 18 car lengths
70 mph (112 km/h)	21 m	75 m	96 metres, 24 car lengths

Key: thinking distance, braking distance

Braking distance

The braking distance of a vehicle can be affected by adverse road and weather conditions and poor condition of the vehicle.

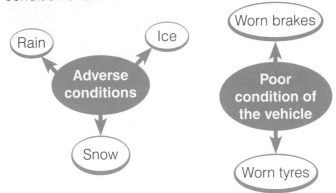

Reaction time

The average reaction time is between 0.2–0.9 seconds but this varies from person to person. Thinking distance increases as speed increases. This is because a faster vehicle travels further during the time taken to react.

A driver's reaction time can be affected by tiredness, drugs and alcohol. Distractions, such as eating, drinking or using a mobile phone, may also affect a driver's ability to react.

A range of different methods can be used to measure reaction times. One example is using a computer programme that flashes a colour or sounds a noise. The participant must then press a key on the keyboard as fast as possible. Average reaction times for this test are often around 0.2–0.3 seconds.

Keywords

Thinking distance ➤ Distance travelled before the driver applies the brakes

Braking distance ➤ Distance a vehicle travels after the brakes have been applied

Braking force

This is what happens when a force is applied to the brakes of a vehicle.

| Work is done by the friction force between the brakes and the wheel. | This reduces the kinetic energy of the vehicle. | The temperature of the brakes increases. |

- ➤ The greater the speed of a vehicle, the greater the braking force needed to stop the vehicle in a certain distance.
- ➤ The greater the braking force, the greater the deceleration of the vehicle.
- ➤ Large decelerations may lead to brakes overheating and / or loss of control.

Design a road safety poster summarising stopping distance, thinking distance, braking distance and all the factors that affect them.

1. What two distances make up the stopping distance?
2. Give two examples of adverse road conditions which can increase the stopping distance.

Momentum

Momentum

Moving objects have **momentum**. Momentum is given by the following equation:

> momentum = mass × velocity
>
> $p = mv$
>
> ➤ momentum, p, in kilograms metre per second, kg m/s
> ➤ mass, m, in kilograms, kg
> ➤ velocity, v, in metres per second, m/s

Example:
A car of mass 1100 kg is travelling at 13 m/s. What is its momentum?

$p = mv$
$= 1100 \times 13$
$= 14\,300$ kg m/s

Conservation of momentum

In a closed system, the total momentum before an event is equal to the total momentum after the event. This is called **conservation of momentum**.

Example:
A cue ball with mass of 0.17 kg travelling at 4 m/s hits a stationary snooker ball with a mass of 0.16 kg. The first ball stops while the other ball starts to move. What is the velocity of the second ball?

Before collision

After collision

momentum = mass × velocity

momentum of first ball before collision $= 0.17 \times 4 = 0.68$ kg m/s

momentum of first ball = 0 (as it is now stationary)
As momentum is the same before and after the collision, the second ball has a momentum of 0.68 kg m/s.

$0.68 = $ mass × velocity
$0.68 = 0.16 \times$ velocity
$\dfrac{0.68}{0.16} = $ velocity
velocity $= 4.25$ m/s

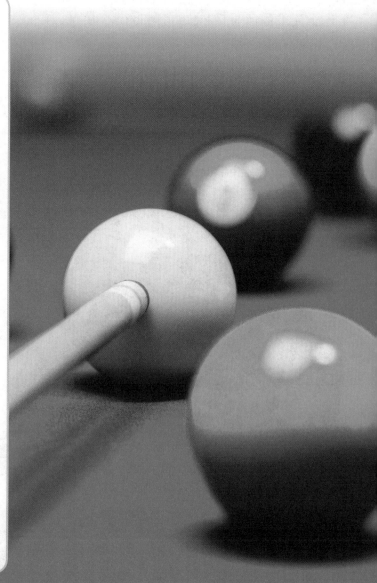

Changes in momentum

When a force acts on an object that is moving or is able to move, a change in momentum occurs.

The equations $F = m \times a$ and

$$a = \frac{v - u}{t}$$

lead to the equation

$$F = \frac{m\Delta v}{\Delta t}$$

➤ $m\Delta v$ = the rate of change of momentum

Example:

When a 20 g dart travelling at 18 m/s hits a dartboard it comes to rest in 0.2 s. What force is generated by this impact?

initial momentum of dart = mass × velocity
$$= 18 \times 0.02$$
$$= 0.36 \text{ kg m/s}$$

final momentum = 0 kg m/s
change in momentum = 0.36 − 0
$$= 0.36$$

$$\text{force} = \frac{\text{the rate of change of momentum}}{\text{time}}$$

$$= \frac{0.36}{0.2}$$

$$= 1.8 \text{ N}$$

Safety features

Safety features include:

➤ airbags
➤ seat belts
➤ gymnasium crash mats
➤ cycle helmets
➤ cushioned surfaces for playgrounds.

All these features slow down the change in momentum in a collision. This reduces the forces on the people involved, reducing injury.

Keyword

Momentum ➤ Product of an object's mass and velocity

Try catching a table tennis ball and then a cricket ball. Note how much harder it is to catch the heavier cricket ball. Use force, mass and momentum to explain this difference.

1. How do airbags reduce the chance of injury in a collision?
2. What is the momentum of an object of 6 kg moving at 4 m/s?
3. What happens to the momentum when a force acts on a moving object?

Mind map

Newton's second law

Newton's first law

Newton's third law

Newton's laws

Conservation of momentum

Momentum

FORCES

Changes in momentum

Safety features

Stopping distance

Thinking distance

Braking distance

Practice questions

1. a) The diagram below shows the forces acting on a stationary bike and rider.

    What is the upward force from the ground? Explain how you arrived at your answer.   **(2 marks)**

    890 N

    b) The diagram on the right shows the same bike and rider moving.

    Is the rider accelerating, decelerating or moving at the same speed? Explain, using Newton's laws, how you arrived at your answer.   **(2 marks)**

    25 N   25 N

    c) A change in terrain caused the friction to increase. What effect would this have on the resultant force and the speed of the rider?   **(2 marks)**

2. A car in a crash test has a total mass of 1200 kg. The car is travelling at a speed of 16 m/s.

    a) The car accelerates at 2.5 m/s². What is its resultant force?   **(2 marks)**

    b) The car maintains a constant speed of 16 m/s. What is the total momentum of the car?   **(3 marks)**

    c) When the car crashes, its momentum becomes zero in 0.4 seconds. What is the force generated by this crash?   **(3 marks)**

    d) Give two safety features that could reduce the risk of injury in a collision like this.   **(2 marks)**

Changes in energy

Keyword
Specific heat capacity ➤ Amount of energy required to raise the temperature of one kilogram of a substance by one degree Celsius

A system is an object or group of objects. When a system changes, the way energy is stored in it also changes.

an object projected upwards, e.g a rocket – chemical energy in the fuel is converted to kinetic energy and gravitational potential energy

bringing water to a boil in an electric kettle – electrical energy to heat and sound energy

Changes

a moving object hitting an obstacle – kinetic energy to sound, heat and kinetic energy

an object accelerated by a constant force, e.g a tennis player hitting a tennis ball – chemical energy in the player to kinetic energy in their arm to kinetic energy in the racket and then kinetic energy in the ball

a vehicle slowing down – kinetic energy to sound and heat energy (friction)

Energy in moving objects

The kinetic energy of a moving object can be calculated using the following equation:

kinetic energy = 0.5 × mass × (speed)²

$$E_k = \frac{1}{2}mv^2$$

➤ kinetic energy, E_k, in joules, J
➤ mass, m, in kilograms, kg
➤ speed, v, in metres per second, m/s

Example:

A ball of mass 0.3 kg falls at 10 m/s. What is the ball's kinetic energy?

$$E_k = \frac{1}{2}mv^2$$
$$= 0.5 \times 0.3 \times 10^2$$
$$= 15 \text{ J}$$

Create a large formula poster with each of the formulas on these pages, a worked example different to the ones on this page and a diagram showing the energy transfer.

Elastic potential energy (E_e)

$$\text{elastic potential energy} = 0.5 \times \text{spring constant} \times \text{extension}^2$$

$$E_e = \frac{1}{2}ke^2$$

(assuming the limit of proportionality has not been exceeded)

➤ elastic potential energy, E_e, in joules, J
➤ spring constant, k, in newtons per metre, N/m
➤ extension, e, in metres, m

Example:

A spring has a spring constant of 500 N/m and is extended by 0.2 m. What is the elastic potential energy in the spring?

$$E_e = \frac{1}{2}ke^2$$
$$= \frac{1}{2}500 \times 0.2^2$$
$$= 250 \times 0.04$$
$$= 10 \text{ J}$$

Changes in thermal energy

The **specific heat capacity** of a substance is the amount of energy required to raise the temperature of one kilogram of the substance by one degree Celsius. The specific heat capacity can be used to calculate the amount of energy stored in or released from a system as its temperature changes. This can be calculated using the following equation:

$$\text{change in thermal energy} = \text{mass} \times \text{specific heat capacity} \times \text{temperature change}$$

$$\Delta E = mc\Delta\theta$$

➤ change in thermal energy, ΔE, in joules, J
➤ mass, m, in kilograms, kg
➤ specific heat capacity, c, in joules per kilogram per degree Celsius, J/kg °C
➤ temperature change, $\Delta\theta$, in degrees Celsius, °C

Example:

0.75 kg of 100°C water cools to 23°C. What is the change in thermal energy?
(Specific heat capacity of water = 4184 J/kg °C)

$$\Delta E = mc\,\Delta\theta$$
$$= 0.75 \times 4184 \times (100 - 23)$$
$$= 241\,626 \text{ J} = 242 \text{ kJ}$$

Gravitational potential energy (g.p.e.)

The amount of gravitational potential energy gained by an object raised above ground level can be calculated using the following equation:

$$\text{g.p.e.} = \text{mass} \times \text{gravitational field strength} \times \text{height}$$

$$E_p = mgh$$

➤ gravitational potential energy, E_p, in joules, J
➤ mass, m, in kilograms, kg
➤ gravitational field strength, g, in newtons per kilogram, N/kg
➤ height, h, in metres, m

Example:

A car of mass 1500 kg drives up a hill which is 67 m high. What is the gravitational potential energy of the car at the top of the hill? (Assume the gravitational field strength is 10 N/kg)

$$E_p = mgh$$
$$= 15\,000 \times 67 \times 10$$
$$= 10\,050 \text{ kJ}$$

1. What is the kinetic energy of a 65 g object travelling at 6 m/s?
2. What is the gravitational potential energy of a 17 kg object at a height of 987 m?
   (gravitational field strength = 10 g)
3. What is specific heat capacity?

Conservation and dissipation of energy

Keyword

Thermal insulation ➤ Material used to reduce transfer of heat energy

Energy transfers in a system

Energy can be **transferred**, **stored** or **dissipated**. It cannot be created or destroyed.

In a closed system there is no net change to the total energy when energy is transferred.

Only part of the energy is usefully transferred. The rest of the energy dissipates and is transferred in less useful ways, often as heat or sound energy. This energy is considered **wasted**.

Examples of processes which cause a rise in temperature and so waste energy as heat include:

➤ friction between the moving parts of a machine

If the energy that is wasted can be reduced, that means more energy can be usefully transferred. The less energy wasted, the more efficient the transfer.

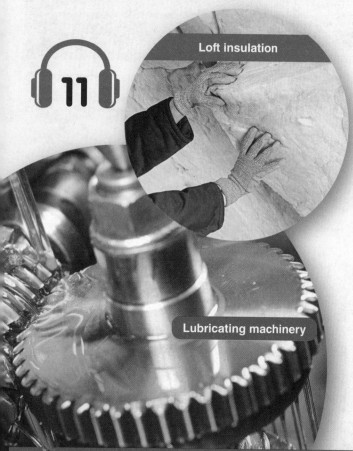

Loft insulation

Lubricating machinery

Efficiency

The energy efficiency for any energy transfer can be calculated using the following equation:

$$\text{efficiency} = \frac{\text{useful output energy transfer}}{\text{total input energy transfer}}$$

Efficiency may also be calculated using the following equation:

$$\text{efficiency} = \frac{\text{useful power}}{\text{total power output}}$$

Example:

Kat uses a hairdryer. Some of the energy is wasted as sound. The electrical energy input is 24 kJ. The energy wasted is 7 kJ. What is the efficiency of the hairdryer?

First calculate the useful energy transferred.

useful energy = total energy – wasted energy
= 24 – 7 = 17 kJ

Now calculate the efficiency.

$$\text{efficiency} = \frac{\text{useful output energy transfer}}{\text{useful input energy transfer}}$$

$$= \frac{17}{24} = 0.71$$

This decimal efficiency can be represented as a percentage by multiplying it by 100.

$$0.71 \times 100 = 71\%$$

There are many ways energy efficiency can be increased:

➤ Lubrication, thermal insulation and low resistance wires reduce energy waste and improve efficiency.

➤ Thermal insulation, such as loft insulation, reduces heat loss.

Example:

Oiling a bike chain reduces friction. This reduces the energy wasted as heat and makes the energy transfer to kinetic energy more efficient.

Power

Power is defined as the rate at which energy is transferred or the rate at which work is done. The power equation is:

$$\text{power} = \frac{\text{work done}}{\text{time}} \qquad P = \frac{W}{T}$$

- ➤ P = power (watts)
- ➤ E = work done (joules)
- ➤ T = time (seconds)

An energy transfer of 1 joule per second is equal to a power of 1 watt.

Example:

A weightlifter is lifting weights that have a mass of 80 kg. What power is required to lift them 2 metres vertically in 4 seconds? (Assume gravitational field strength of 10 N/kg)

$$\text{power} = \frac{\text{work done}}{\text{time}}$$

$$\text{work done} = \text{force} \times \text{distance}$$
$$\text{force} = \text{mass} \times \text{gravitational field strength}$$
$$= 80 \times 10 = 800 \text{ N}$$

$$\text{work done} = 800 \times 2 = 1600 \text{ J}$$

$$\text{power} = \frac{1600}{4} = 800 \text{ W}$$

A second weightlifter lifted the same mass to the same height in 3 seconds. As he carried out the same amount of work but in a shorter time, he would have a greater power.

Thermal insulation

Thermal insulation has a low thermal conductivity, so has a slow rate of energy transfer by conduction. U-values give a measure of the heat loss through a substance. A higher U-value indicates that a material has a higher thermal conductivity.

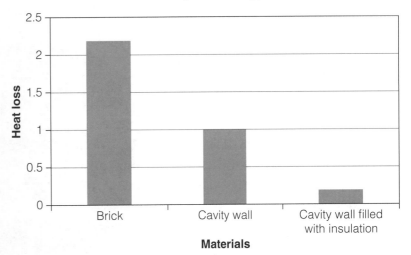

Changing the material of walls to materials that have a lower thermal conductivity reduces heat loss (the U-value) and so a building cools more slowly, reducing heating costs. The graph below shows the heat lost by different types of wall.

Increasing the thickness of walls could also reduce heat loss. The house below is not fitted with insulation, so lots of heat is being lost through the walls due to their high thermal conductivity. This can be seen by the red/orange colour on the infrared image.

Record all the energy that is wasted from appliances you use in a day. What do you think are the most wasteful appliances? (Hint: they're likely to be the ones that are noisy or get hot.)

1. Why is it important to increase the efficiency of an energy transfer?
2. A washing machine transfers 400 J of useful energy out of a total of 652 J. What is the efficiency of the washing machine?
3. What effect does fitting cavity wall insulation have on the thermal conductivity of the building's wall?

National and global energy resources

Keywords
Renewable ➤ Energy resource that can be replenished as it is used
Non-renewable ➤ Energy resource that will eventually run out

Energy resources

Energy resources are used for transport, electricity generation and heating.

Energy resources can be divided into **renewable** and **non-renewable**. Renewable resources can be replenished as they are used. Non-renewable energy resources will eventually run out.

Renewable	Non-renewable
➤ Bio-fuel	➤ Coal
➤ Wind	➤ Oil
➤ Hydro-electricity	➤ Gas
➤ Geothermal	➤ Nuclear fuel
➤ Tidal power	
➤ Solar power	
➤ Water waves	

Non-renewable

Renewable

Reliability

Fossil fuels (coal, oil and gas) and nuclear fuel are very reliable as they can always be used to release energy. Fossil fuels are burnt to release the stored chemical energy, and nuclear fuel radiates energy.

The wind and the Sun are examples of energy resources that are not very reliable, as the wind doesn't always blow and it's not always sunny.

All the energy resources in the table on the opposite page can be used to generate electricity. The following energy resources can be used for transport and heating.

Coal

Oil

Heating

Coal – steam trains

Wind – ships with sails

Transport

Solar – experimental solar-powered cars and planes are currently being tested

Natural Gas

Oil – can be used to make petrol, diesel and jet fuel

Nuclear – submarines

Ethical and environmental concerns

➤ Burning fossil fuels produces carbon dioxide, which is a greenhouse gas. Increased greenhouse gas emissions are leading to climate change. Particulates and other pollutants are also released, which cause respiratory problems.

➤ Nuclear power produces hazardous nuclear waste and also has the potential for nuclear accidents, with devastating health and environmental consequences.

➤ Some people consider wind turbines to be ugly and to spoil the landscape.

➤ Building tidal power stations can lead to the destruction of important tidal habitats.

In recent years, there have been attempts to move away from over-reliance on fossil fuels to renewable forms of energy. However, fossil fuels are still used to deliver the vast majority of our energy needs.

Write out each of the different energy resources on cards, then mix the cards up and sort them into two piles: renewable and non-renewable.

1. Give three examples of renewable energy resources and three examples of non-renewable energy resources.
2. Why aren't solar and wind power reliable energy resources?
3. What is an environmental concern about burning fossil fuels?

Mind map

Efficiency

Thermal insulation

Stored

Kinetic energy

Dissipation

Transferred

Elastic potential energy

Changes in energy

Power

Specific heat capacity

ENERGY

Gravitational potential energy

Work

Global energy

Power

Non-renewable

Renewable

Practice questions

1. a) Explain the difference between a renewable and a non-renewable energy resource. **(2 marks)**

    b) Nuclear power is a very reliable source of energy but some environmentalists
        protest against it.
        Explain why. **(2 marks)**

    c) Many environmentalists would rather use wind or tidal power stations.
        What are the potential disadvantages of using these energy resources? **(2 marks)**

2. A car has a mass of 1600 kg and moves at 32 m/s.

    a) What is the kinetic energy of the car? **(2 marks)**

    b) If the fuel burnt by the car to reach this speed contained 1500 kJ, what was the efficiency
        of this transfer of energy? **(2 marks)**

    c) Give two ways energy was transferred into less useful forms by the car's engine. **(2 marks)**

    d) Give one feature of the car's engine that reduced the energy dissipated. **(1 mark)**

3. A bungee jumper of mass 77 kg stands on a bridge 150 m high.

    a) What is their gravitational potential energy? (Assume gravitational field strength = 10 N/kg) **(2 marks)**

    b) The bungee jumper jumps off and quickly reaches a speed of 20 m/s.
        What is their kinetic energy at this point? **(2 marks)**

    c) Explain the energy transfers that occur from when the bungee jumper jumps to
        when they reach their lowest height. **(2 marks)**

Transverse and longitudinal waves

Waves may be either transverse or longitudinal.

Transverse waves

In a transverse wave, the oscillations are perpendicular to the direction of energy transfer, such as the ripples on the surface of water.

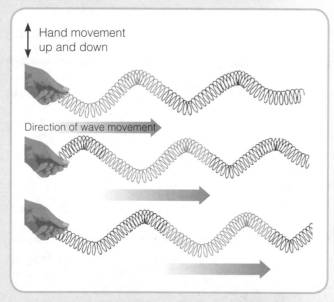

Hand movement up and down

Direction of wave movement

Longitudinal waves

In a longitudinal wave, the oscillations are parallel to the direction of energy transfer. Longitudinal waves show areas of **compression** and **rarefaction**, such as sound waves travelling through air.

Hand movement in and out

Compression

Expansion (rarefaction)

Direction of wave movement

Wave movement

In both sound waves in air and ripples on the water surface, it is the wave that moves forward rather than the air or water molecules. The waves transfer energy and information without transferring matter.

This can be shown experimentally. For example, when a tuning fork is used to create a sound wave that moves out from the fork, the air particles don't move away from the fork. (This would create a vacuum around the tuning fork.)

Properties of waves

Waves are described by their:

➤ **amplitude** – The amplitude of a wave is the maximum displacement of a point on a wave away from its undisturbed position.
➤ **wavelength** – The wavelength of a wave is the distance from a point on one wave to the equivalent point on the adjacent wave.
➤ **frequency** – The frequency of a wave is the number of waves passing a point each second.
➤ **period** – The time for one complete wave to pass a fixed point. The equation for the time period (T) of a wave is given by the following equation:

$$\text{period} = \frac{1}{\text{frequency}}$$

$$\text{period} = \frac{1}{f}$$

➤ period, T, in seconds, s

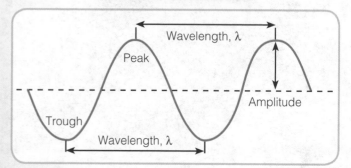

Wavelength, λ

Peak

Amplitude

Trough

Wavelength, λ

Wave speed

The wave speed is the speed at which the energy is transferred (or the wave moves) through the medium.

The wave speed is given by the following wave equation:

wave speed = frequency × wavelength

$$v = f\lambda$$

➤ wave speed, v, in metres per second, m/s

➤ frequency, f, in hertz, Hz

➤ wavelength, λ, in metres, m

Example:

A sound wave in air has a frequency of 250 Hz and a wavelength of 1.32 m. What is the speed of the sound wave?

wave speed = frequency × wavelength

           = 250 × 1.32

           = 330 m/s

A ripple tank and a stroboscope can be used to measure the speed of ripples on the surface of water.

As wave speed, frequency and wavelength are all interrelated, changes in wave speed due to waves travelling between different media will affect the wavelength of a sound. For example, when sound waves enter a more dense medium, the wave speed increases. This leads to an increase in the sound's wavelength.

Make a series of cards with the names of key properties of a wave on one side and their definitions on the other. Use these cards for revision and to test yourself.

1. Give an example of a longitudinal wave and an example of a transverse wave.
2. Define the term 'wavelength'.
3. A sound wave travels in air at a speed of 343 m/s at a frequency of 90 Hz. The sound wave enters seawater where its speed increases to 1500 m/s. If the frequency of the water remains constant, what is the effect on the wavelength?

When a wave reaches a boundary between two different materials, the waves can be **absorbed** (energy transferred to the matter), **transmitted** (passed through the material) or **reflected**.

Sound waves and reflection of waves

14

Reflection

The ray diagram right shows the **reflection** of a wave from a surface.

➤ The incident ray is the incoming ray and the reflected ray is created by the reflection.
➤ The normal is a line perpendicular to the reflecting surface at the point where the incident ray hits the surface.
➤ The **angle of incidence** is the angle between the incident ray and the normal.
➤ The **angle of reflection** is the angle between the reflected ray and the normal.
➤ The angle of incidence = the angle of reflection.
➤ If the angle of incidence of the wave is above the critical angle, all the waves reflect back. This is **total internal reflection**.

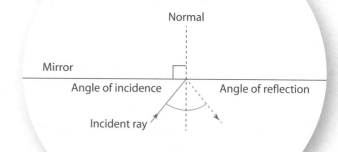

Normal

Mirror

Angle of incidence   Angle of reflection

Incident ray

Sound waves

Sound waves can travel through solids causing vibrations in the solid.

Within the ear, sound waves cause the ear drum and other parts to vibrate. These vibrations are transmitted to the brain by the nervous system and are perceived as sounds.

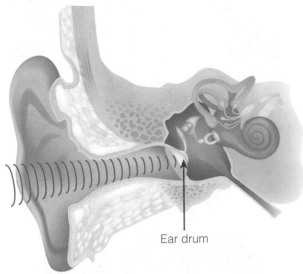

Ear drum

The conversion of sound waves to vibrations of solids works over a limited frequency range. Sounds outside this frequency range do not cause vibrations of the ear parts. As the ear parts do not vibrate, no signal is transmitted to the brain and therefore no sound is heard.

This means that the range of normal human hearing is from 20 Hz to 20 kHz. Sounds over 20 kHz are known as **ultrasound**.

Measuring the speed of sound

The speed of sound in air can be measured in a number of ways.

One simple method is to stand a long distance from a wall that produces an echo, clap and then record how long it takes to hear the echo. The speed of sound can then be calculated using this time and distance from the wall.

As we're hearing an echo, the sound is travelling twice the distance to the wall (to the wall and back again).

For example, if you are standing 60m from the wall:

Time taken to hear echo = 0.36s

Distance from wall = 60 x 2 = 120m

Speed of sound $= \dfrac{120}{0.36} = 333$m/s

The speed of sound can also be measured using a data logger linked to two microphones that are set a distance apart. A sound will reach the two microphones at different times. The time difference and the distance between the two microphones can be used to calculate the speed of sound.

Hold a small mirror vertical. Rotate the mirror until you can see yourself in it and then use a protractor to measure the angle the mirror has moved. Now repeat the experiment with the mirror a different distance from you. Does distance have an effect on the angle?

1. What does the angle of incidence equal?
2. Name a part of the ear that vibrates and allows sound to be perceived.
3. What is the normal frequency range of human hearing?

Waves for detection and exploration

HT

Waves

Different types of waves have different velocities, absorption and reflection in solids and liquids. This means that waves can be used both for detection and exploration of structures that are hidden from direct observation.

Ultrasound

Ultrasound waves have a frequency higher than the upper limit of hearing for humans.

Ultrasound waves are partially reflected when they meet a boundary between two different media. The time taken for the reflections to reach a detector can be used to determine how far away such a boundary is. This allows ultrasound waves to be used for both medical and industrial imaging.

One of the major uses of ultrasound is prenatal scans.

Write each of the wave types featured in this module on cards. On different cards write what they're used to detect. On a third set of cards write why the waves are suitable for this type of detection. Mix all the cards up and then rearrange them into the correct order.

Keyword

Ultrasound ➤ Longitudinal waves with a frequency higher than the upper limit of hearing for humans

Earthquakes

Earthquakes produce two types of seismic wave that travel through the Earth:

1. P-waves are longitudinal, seismic waves. P-waves travel at different speeds through solids and liquids.

2. S-waves are transverse, seismic waves. S-waves cannot travel through a liquid.

P-waves and S-waves have been used to provide evidence for the structure and size of the Earth's core. As it is impossible to see the internal structure of the Earth, we must use models to study it.

P-waves and S-waves are detected on the Earth's surface. Only P-waves are detected on the opposite side of the Earth from the epicentre of the earthquake, not S-waves. This helps prove that the outer core of the Earth is liquid, preventing the passage of S-waves.

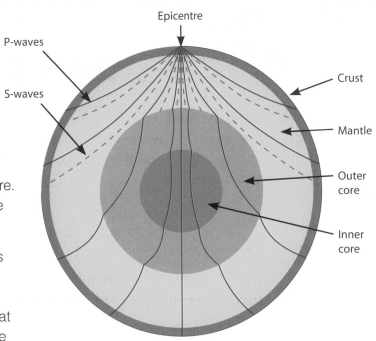

Echo sounding

Echo sounding (sonar) using high frequency sound waves is used to detect objects in deep water and to measure water depth.

Fishing vessels use echo sounding to detect shoals of fish. The high frequency sound bounces off the group of fish and is detected by the boat. The time interval between the ultrasound being produced and detected allows the distance to the fish shoal to be determined.

Example:

A fishing boat releases high frequency sound waves and detects the reflection from a shoal of fish 0.5 seconds later. The speed of sound in water is 1500 m/s. How far below the boat are the fish?

$$\text{distance} = \text{speed} \times \text{time}$$
$$= 1500 \times 0.5$$
$$= 750 \text{ metres}$$
$$= \frac{750}{2}$$
$$= 375 \text{ metres}$$

This value then needs to be divided by 2 as this is how far the sound waves must travel to the fish shoal and then back to the boat.

---

1. Give two differences between P-waves and S-waves.
2. Give one similarity and one difference between the use of ultrasound and echo sounding.
3. Why are S-waves not detected on the opposite point of the Earth's surface from an earthquake's epicentre?

Electromagnetic waves and properties 1

Electromagnetic waves

Electromagnetic waves are transverse waves that:

➤ transfer energy from the source of the waves to an absorber

➤ form a continuous spectrum

➤ travel at the same velocity through a vacuum (space) or air.

The waves that form the electromagnetic spectrum are grouped in terms of their wavelength and their frequency.

The electromagnetic spectrum

Low frequency   High frequency

Radio waves | Micro-waves | Infrared radiation | Visible light | Ultraviolet | X-rays | Gamma rays

10^3 m   1 m 10^{-3} m 10^{-5} m 10^{-7} m 10^{-9} m 10^{-11} m 10^{-13} m

Wavelength

Visible light

> **HT** Different substances may absorb, transmit, refract or reflect electromagnetic waves in ways that vary with wavelength.

Human eyes only detect visible light so only identify a limited range of electromagnetic radiation.

| | Radio waves | | | Infrared | Ultra-violet | X-rays | Gamma rays |
| AM | FM | TV | Radar | | | | |

100 m   1 m   1 cm   0.01 cm   1000 nm   10 nm   0.01 nm   0.0001 nm

Visible light

Visible spectrum

700 nm   600 nm   500 nm   400 nm

Wavelength

Refraction

Refraction is when a wave changes direction as it travels from one medium to another.

Refraction occurs due to the wave changing speed as it moves between media. Waves have different velocities in different media.

Light refraction through water

In the example above, the fish appears to be above its actual position due to the refraction of the light rays. Light travels faster in the air than it does in the water. This leads to the light ray bending away from the normal. When light slows down, it bends towards the normal.

The wave front diagram below shows a wave moving from air (less optically dense) to water (more optically dense). As the wave travels slower in a denser medium, the edge of the wave that hits the water first slows down whilst the rest of the wave continues at the same speed. This causes the light to bend towards the normal. The opposite effect occurs when a wave moves from a more optically dense medium to a less optically dense medium.

Keyword

HT Refraction ➤ Change in direction of a wave as it travels from one medium to another

Light rays travelling through water

Write each of the different types of electromagnetic radiation on separate cards. Mix them up and then rearrange them into the correct order, from largest wavelength to smallest wavelength.

1. Which has the largest wavelength: infrared radiation or ultraviolet radiation?
2. What section of electromagnetic radiation can be perceived by the human eye?
3. **HT** Which way do waves bend when they enter a more optically dense medium?

Electromagnetic waves and properties 2

Keyword
Gamma rays ➤ Electromagnetic radiation that originates from changes in the nucleus
Sievert ➤ Unit of radiation dose

Electromagnetic waves

Changes in atoms and the nuclei of atoms can result in electromagnetic waves being generated or absorbed over a wide frequency range.

Gamma rays originate from changes in the nucleus of an atom.

HT Radio waves

Radio waves can be produced by oscillations in electrical circuits. When radio waves are absorbed they may create an alternating current with the same frequency as the radio wave. Therefore, radio waves induce oscillations in an electrical circuit.

The diagram below shows the main features of electromagnetic waves.

Ultraviolet waves, x-rays and gamma rays can have hazardous effects on human body tissue.

The effects of electromagnetic waves depend on the type of radiation and the size of the dose.

1000 millisieverts (mSv) equals 1 sievert (Sv)

Radiation dose (in **sieverts**) is a measure of the risk of harm from an exposure of the body to the radiation.

Ultraviolet waves can cause skin to age prematurely and increase the risk of skin cancer.

X-rays and gamma rays are ionising radiation that can cause the mutation of genes and cancer.

Make separate cards of the names of each electromagnetic radiation, its uses and any associated dangers. Mix up all these cards and then match them up.

Uses of electromagnetic waves

Electromagnetic waves have many practical applications.

Radio waves	Television, radio	Low frequency radio waves can diffract around hills and reflect off the ionosphere, meaning they don't require a direct line of sight between transmitter and receiver.
Microwaves	Satellite communications, cooking food	Their small wavelength allows them to be directed in narrow beams.
Infrared	Electrical heaters, cooking food, infrared cameras	Thermal radiation heats up objects.
Visible light	Fibre optic communications	This can be reflected down a fibre optic cable.
Ultraviolet	Energy efficient lamps, sun tanning	Ultraviolet is used for low energy light bulbs to produce white light. This requires less energy than filament bulbs.
X-rays	Medical imaging and treatments	X-rays are absorbed differently by different parts of the body; more are absorbed by hard tissues, such as bone, and less are absorbed by soft tissues. This allows images of the inside of the body to be created.
Gamma rays	Medical imaging and treatment of cancer	Gamma rays can be used to destroy cancerous tumours and carry out functional organ scans.

HT **1.** How are radio waves produced?

2. What are the potential dangers of gamma rays?

3. Give one use of ultraviolet radiation.

Lenses and visible light

Lenses

A lens forms an image by refracting light.

➤ Convex lens – parallel rays of light are brought to a focus at the principal focus. Convex lenses can form virtual or real images.

➤ Concave lens – parallel rays of light diverge when they pass through a concave lens. Concave lenses always form virtual images.

Real images and virtual images

The distance from the lens to the principal focus is called the **focal length**.

The effect of convex and concave lenses can be shown by ray diagrams. The lenses will be represented by symbols.

Convex lens   **Concave lens**

The magnification produced by a lens can be calculated using the following equation:

$$\text{magnification} = \frac{\text{image height}}{\text{object height}}$$

Magnification is a ratio and so has no limits.

Image heights and object heights are usually measured in mm or cm.

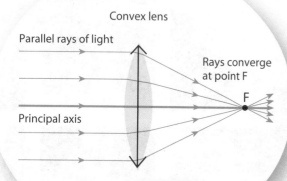

Convex lens

Parallel rays of light

Rays converge at point F

F

Principal axis

> **Example:**
> What is the magnification of an image that is 8 cm high when the original object was 0.3 cm high?
>
> $$\text{magnification} = \frac{\text{image height}}{\text{object height}}$$
> $$= \frac{8}{0.3}$$
> $$= 27 \times \text{magnification}$$

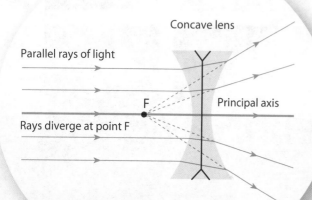

Concave lens

Parallel rays of light

F   Principal axis

Rays diverge at point F

Keywords

Opaque ➤ Object that reflects light

Transparent ➤ Object that allows all light to pass through

Translucent ➤ Object that diffuses the light that passes through it, meaning that things observed through a translucent material are not properly visible

Visible light

Each colour within the visible light spectrum has a narrow range of wavelengths and frequency.

λ [nm] 780   700   600   500   380

Opaque objects reflect or absorb all light incident on them. The colour of an opaque object is determined by which wavelengths of light are more strongly reflected. Wavelengths not reflected are absorbed.

For example, a blue object absorbs all wavelengths of visible light except blue. The blue wavelength is diffusely reflected into the eyes of the observer.

A white object reflects all wavelengths of light equally, so the object appears white.

White object

A black object absorbs all wavelengths of light (no reflection occurs).

Black object

A blue object absorbs all wavelengths of light except blue which it reflects. It therefore appears blue.

Blue object

There are two types of reflection:

➤ Specular reflection – reflection from a smooth surface in a single direction, e.g. reflection from a mirror.

➤ Diffuse reflection – reflection from a rough surface causes scattering. Diffuse reflection allows us to see objects.

Objects that transmit light are either **transparent** (allow all light to pass through) or **translucent** (allow light through but diffuses it, causing things observed through a translucent object to not be properly visible).

Colour filters are transparent objects that transmit certain wavelengths of light and absorb all other wavelengths of light. For example, a red filter transmits red light and absorbs all other visible light wavelengths.

Red filter

On separate cards, write 'Specular reflection', 'Diffuse reflection', 'Opaque', 'Translucent' and 'Transparent'. Now write the definitions of each of these key terms on separate cards and draw diagrams to represent them on separate cards. Mix the cards up and then match the terms to the diagrams and descriptions.

1. What type of image is formed by a concave lens?
2. What light is transmitted by a blue filter?
3. What is the original height of an object that has been magnified 4 times to produce a 17 cm high image?

Black body radiation

Keyword

Emission ➤ Release of energy

Emission and absorption of infrared radiation

All bodies **emit** and absorb infrared radiation. The hotter the body, the more infrared radiation it emits in a given time.

A perfect black body is a theoretical object that:

➤ absorbs all of the radiation incident on it
➤ does not reflect or transmit any radiation
➤ is the best possible emitter as it emits the maximum amount of radiation possible at a given temperature.

A perfect black body is impossible in the real world as no object can fulfil these criteria.

All bodies emit radiation, and the intensity and wavelength distribution of any emission depends on the temperature of the body.

A body at a constant temperature is absorbing radiation at the same rate as it is emitting radiation. The temperature of a body increases when the body absorbs radiation faster than it emits radiation.

The temperature of the Earth depends on many factors including:

➤ the rates of absorption of radiation
➤ the rate of emission of radiation
➤ the rate of reflection of radiation into space.

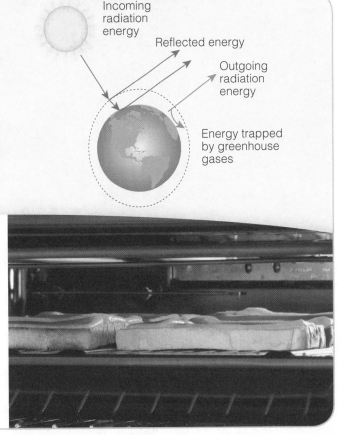

Incoming radiation energy

Reflected energy

Outgoing radiation energy

Energy trapped by greenhouse gases

The temperature of a body is related to the radiation absorbed and the radiation emitted.

For example, when food is beneath a grill it is absorbing more radiation than it is emitting so its temperature is increased. When the food is removed from the grill, it now emits more radiation than it is absorbing. This means the food cools down.

Create a large flow diagram showing energy being absorbed, released and emitted from the Earth. Include as many energy sources as you can.

1. Give the three main characteristics of a perfect black body.
HT 2. Give two factors the temperature of the Earth depends on.
HT 3. What will happen to the temperature of a body that is emitting as much radiation as it is absorbing?

Mind map

Echo sounding

Ultrasound

Compression

Sound waves

Wave speed

Rarefaction

P-waves

Longitudinal

Refraction

WAVES

Hazards

Reflection

Electromagnetic spectrum

Transverse

Uses

S-waves

Infrared radiation

Visible light

Perfect black body

Lenses

Convex

Concave

Practice questions

1. How does compression differ from rarefaction? **(2 marks)**

2. What is the frequency of a wave travelling at 200 m/s with a wavelength of 3.2 m? **(2 marks)**

3. Explain how P-waves and S-waves from an earthquake can be used to draw conclusions about the structure of the Earth. **(4 marks)**

4. A 5 cm high image is formed by a magnification of 2.2.

   What is the height of the original object? **(2 marks)**

5. Look at the ray diagram below.

Principal axis

F

   a) What type of lens is shown in the diagram above? **(1 mark)**

   b) Complete the ray diagram to show the effect of the lens. **(1 mark)**

6. What does the colour of green plants suggest about what light is reflected and absorbed by them? **(2 marks)**

7. David wrote the following explanation of how sound travels:

   'Sound travels as a transverse wave. When a sound wave travels in air the oscillations of the air particles are perpendicular to the direction of energy transfer. The sound wave transfers matter and energy.'

   Write this paragraph out again, correcting the three mistakes David has made. **(3 marks)**

8. How can sonar be used to detect shoals of fish? **(3 marks)**

Circuits, charge and current

Circuit symbols

The diagram below shows the standard symbols used for components in a circuit.

Here is an example of a circuit diagram:

Cell		Lamp		
Battery		Diode		
Switch (open)				
Switch (closed)		LED		
Voltmeter	V	Thermistor		
LDR		Resistor		
Variable resistor		Ammeter	A	
		Fuse		

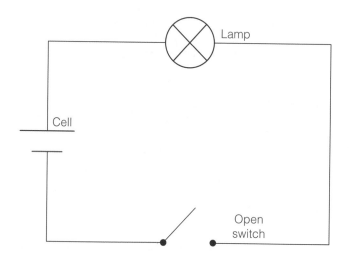

Lamp

Cell

Open switch

Resistors

Fuses

Diodes

Switches

Keyword

Electric current ➤ Flow of electrical charge

AMPERES

Electrical charge and current

For electrical charge to flow through a closed circuit, the circuit must include a source of energy that produces a potential difference, such as a battery, cell or powerpack.

Electric current is a flow of electrical charge. The size of the electric current is the rate of flow of electrical charge. Charge flow, current and time are linked by the following equation:

> **charge flow = current × time**
>
> $$Q = It$$
>
> ➤ charge flow, Q, in coulombs, C
> ➤ current, I, in amperes or amps A
> ➤ time, t, in seconds, s

Example:

A current of 6 A flows through a circuit for 14 seconds. What is the charge flow?

charge flow = current × time
= 6 × 14
= 84 C

The current at any point in a single closed loop of a circuit has the same value as the current at any other point in the same closed loop.

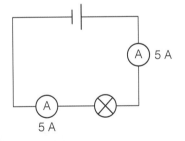

Both ammeters in the circuit above show the same current of 5 amps.

Create flash cards of each of the circuit symbols. Draw the symbol on one side of the card and the name of the symbol on the other. Use these cards to test yourself at naming the symbols.

1. What is the difference between the symbol for a resistor and the symbol for a variable resistor?
2. What charge flows through a circuit per second if the current is 4.2 A?
3. What is the current of a charge flow of 450 C in five seconds?

Current, resistance and potential difference

Current, resistance and potential difference

The current through a component depends on both the resistance of the component and the potential difference (p.d.) across the component.

The greater the resistance of the component, the smaller the current for a given potential difference across the component.

Current, potential difference or resistance can be calculated using the following equation:

> **potential difference = current × resistance**
>
> $$V = IR$$
>
> ➤ potential difference, *V*, in volts, V
> ➤ current, *I*, in amperes or amps, A
> ➤ resistance, *R*, in ohms, Ω

Example:

A 5 ohm resistor has a current of 2 A flowing through it. What is the potential difference across the resistor?

potential difference = current × resistance
$$= 5 \times 2$$
$$= 10 \text{ V}$$

By measuring the current through, and potential difference across a component, it's possible to calculate the resistance of a component.

The circuit diagram below would allow you to determine the resistance of the filament lamp.

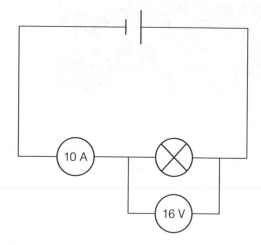

potential difference = current × resistance

$$\text{resistance} = \frac{\text{potential difference}}{\text{current}}$$

$$= \frac{16}{10}$$

$$= 1.6 \text{ ohms}$$

Create a circuit using coloured wool or string – include at least six different components. Stick it onto a large sheet of paper and then annotate it.

Keyword

Ohmic conductor ➤ Resistor at constant temperature where the current is directly proportional to the potential difference

Resistors

For some resistors, the value of R remains constant but in others (e.g. variable resistors) R can change as the current changes.

In an **ohmic conductor**, at a constant temperature the current is directly proportional to the potential difference across the resistor. This means that the resistance remains constant as the current changes.

The resistance of components such as lamps, diodes, thermistors and LDRs is not constant; it changes with the current through the component. They are not ohmic conductors.

Filament lamps

The resistance of a filament lamp increases as the temperature of the filament increases.

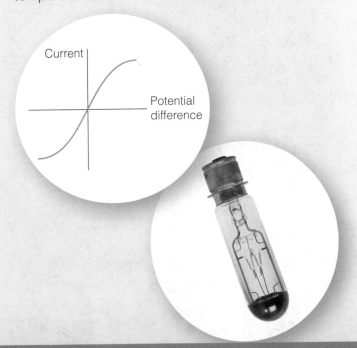

Diodes

The current through a diode flows in one direction only. This means the diode has a very high resistance in the reverse direction.

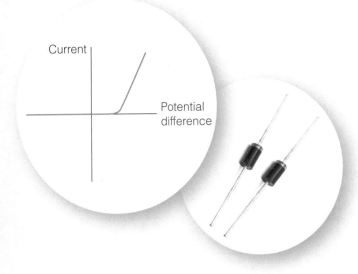

Light dependent resistors (LDR)

The resistance of an LDR decreases as light intensity increases. LDRs are used in circuits where lights are required to switch on when it gets dark, such as floodlights.

Thermistors

The resistance of a thermistor decreases as the temperature increases. Thermistors are used in thermostats to control heating systems.

🎧 21

1. Explain why an LDR is not an ohmic conductor.
2. What two pieces of equipment need to be wired into a circuit in order to determine the resistance of a component in the circuit?
3. What is the potential difference if the current is 4 A and the resistance is 2 ohms?
4. Calculate the resistance of a component that has a current of 3 A flowing through it and a potential difference of 6 V.

Components can be joined together in either a **series circuit** or a **parallel circuit**. Some circuits can include both series and parallel sections.

Series and parallel circuits

Voltmeter

Series circuits

6 V

A) 2 A

A
2 A

V
3 V

V
3 V

For components connected in series:
➤ there is the same current through each component
➤ the total potential difference of the power supply is shared between the components
➤ the total resistance of two components is the sum of the resistance of each component.

Total resistance is given by the following equation:

$R\text{ total} = R1 + R2$
➤ resistance, R, in ohms, Ω

Example:
What is the total resistance of the two resistors in the series circuit below?

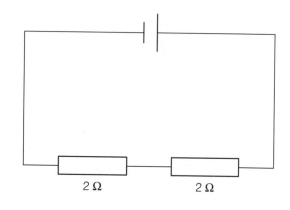

2 Ω   2 Ω

Total = R1 + R2
= 2 Ω + 2 Ω
= 4 Ω

Keywords
Series circuit ➤ Circuit where all components are connected along a single path
Parallel circuit ➤ Circuit which contains branches and where all the components will have the same voltage

Parallel circuits

For components connected in parallel:

➤ the potential difference across each component is the same

➤ the total current through the whole circuit is the sum of the currents through the separate components. The current splits between the branches of the circuit and combines when the branches meet

➤ the total resistance of two resistors is less than the resistance of the smallest individual resistor. This is due to the potential difference across the resistors being the same but the current splitting.

Draw a parallel circuit of your own design, making sure that you include at least two resistors.

1. If the current through one component in a series circuit is 5 A, what is the current through the rest of the components?
2. How do you calculate the total resistance of two resistors in series?
3. A 3 Ω resistor and a 2 Ω resistor are connected in parallel. Would the resistance be higher or lower than 2 Ω?

23

Domestic uses and safety

Mains electricity

WS Most electrical appliances are connected to the mains using a three-core cable with a three-pin plug.

Live wire	Brown	Carries the alternating potential difference from the supply.
Neutral wire	Blue	Completes the circuit. The neutral wire is at, or close to, earth potential (0 V).
Earth wire	Green and yellow stripes	The earth wire is a safety wire to stop the appliance becoming live and is at 0 V. It only carries a current if there is a fault.

Direct and alternating potential difference

Cells and batteries supply current that always passes in the same direction. This is direct current (**dc**). This means the potential difference remains constant. For example, a 9 V battery supplies 9V continuously.

The current of mains electricity changes direction. This is alternating current (**ac**). Mains electricity in the UK has a frequency of 50 Hz – this means that the current changes direction fifty times per second. This causes the potential difference of a live mains wire to vary between a large positive voltage and a large negative voltage. The mean potential difference of the UK mains supply is about 230 V.

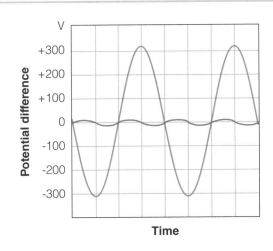

The graph shows the potential difference of two wires in a UK mains electricity cable. The red line shows the changes in potential difference in the live wire. The blue line shows the neutral wire, which has a potential difference of 0V. The mean potential difference is 230V but peaks and troughs of the live wire are greater than 230V.

The potential difference between the live wire and earth (0 V) is about 230 V.

Our bodies are at earth potential (0 V). Touching a live wire produces a large potential difference across our body. This causes a current to flow through our body, resulting in an electric shock that could cause serious injury or death.

Keywords

dc ➤ Direct current that always passes in the same direction

ac ➤ Alternating current that changes direction

A live wire may be dangerous even when a switch in the mains circuit is open.

The fuse in a plug provides protection if a fault occurs. In the event of a fault, a large current flows from the live wire to earth. This melts the fuse and disconnects the live wire. Devices called circuit breakers work in a similar way. They respond more rapidly than a fuse to current changes – this makes them safer and they can be reset once the fault has been corrected.

Circuit breaker

Make small cards of the colours, names and functions of the wires in a three-pin plug. Mix the cards up and then arrange them to show the correct colours, functions and names of the wires.

1. What colour is the neutral wire?
2. What is the function of the earth wire?
3. Why is it dangerous to touch a live wire?

24

Keyword

National Grid ➤ System of transformers and cables linking power stations to consumers

Power

The power transfer in any circuit device is related to the potential difference across it and the current through it, and to the energy changes over time. Power can be calculated using the following equations.

> **power = potential difference × current**
>
> $$P = VI$$
>
> or
>
> **power = current² × resistance**
>
> $$P = I^2 R$$
>
> ➤ power, P, in watts, W
> ➤ potential difference, V, in volts, V
> ➤ current, I, in amperes or amps, A
> ➤ resistance, R, in ohms, Ω

Example:

A bulb has a potential difference of 240 V and a current flowing through it of 0.6 A. What is the power of the bulb?

power = potential difference × current
$$= 240 \times 0.6$$
$$= 144 \text{ W}$$

Energy transfers in everyday appliances

Everyday electrical appliances are designed to bring about energy transfers.

The amount of energy an appliance transfers depends on how long the appliance is switched on for and the power of the appliance.

Here are some examples of everyday energy transfer in appliances:

➤ A hairdryer transfers electrical energy from the ac mains to kinetic energy (in an electric motor to drive a fan) and heat energy (in a heating element).

➤ A torch transfers electrical energy from batteries into light energy from a bulb.

➤ A hair dryer will have a much greater power (2200W) than a battery powered torch (10W). The hair dryer is therefore transferring much more electrical energy than a torch over a given time.

Work done

Work is done when charge flows in a circuit.

The amount of energy transferred by electrical work can be calculated using the following equation:

> **energy transferred = power × time**
>
> $$E = Pt$$
>
> **and**
>
> **energy transferred = charge flow × potential difference**
>
> $$E = QV$$
>
> ➤ energy transferred, *E*, in joules, J
> ➤ power, *P*, in watts, W
> ➤ time, *t*, in seconds, s,
> ➤ charge flow, *Q*, in coulombs, C
> ➤ potential difference, *V*, in volts, V

The National Grid

The **National Grid** is a system of cables and transformers linking power stations to consumers.

Electrical power is transferred from power stations to consumers using the National Grid.

Step-up transformers **increase** the potential difference from the power station to the transmission cables.

Step-down transformers **decrease** the potential difference to a much lower and safer level for domestic use.

Increasing the potential difference reduces the current so reduces the energy loss due to heating in the transmission cables. Reducing the loss of energy through heat makes the transfer of energy much more efficient. Also, the wires would glow and be more likely to break over time if the current through them was high.

Make a flow chart showing the transfer of electrical energy into other forms of energy that occur during your day (TV, computer, mobile, hairdryer and so on).

1. What is the power of a device that has a current flowing through it of 5 A and a resistance of 2 Ω?
2. What is the energy transferred by a charge flow of 60 C and a potential difference of 12 V?
3. Why are step-down transformers important in the National Grid?

Static electricity

Keyword
Static electricity ➤ Imbalance of electrical charges on or in a material

25

Static charge

When certain insulating materials are rubbed against each other they become electrically charged.

Electrons are rubbed off one material and on to the other. As electrons are negatively charged, the material that gains electrons becomes negatively charged. The material that loses electrons has an equal positive charge.

As the charge remains on the materials, this is **static electricity**. These materials now have become electrically charged. This is a static charge.

If two objects that carry the same type of charge are brought together, they repel. For example, two positively charged objects will repel.

Two objects that carry different types of charge will attract. For example, a positively charged object will attract a negatively charged object.

Electron

Attraction and repulsion between two charged objects are examples of non-contact forces.

If this potential difference becomes high enough, a spark may jump across the gap between the object and an earthed conductor brought near to it.

Electric fields

A charged object creates an electric field around itself. An electrical field is a region where an electrical charge experiences a force. The electric field is strongest close to the charged object. The further away from the charged object, the weaker the field. The number and density of field lines show the strength of the field – the more lines, the stronger the field.

A second charged object placed in the field experiences a force. The force gets stronger as the distance between the objects decreases.

This force is the attraction and repulsion felt by charged objects when they are brought together. The field lines show the direction the force would act on a positively charged object. The electrical field is also what leads to the sparking between charged objects.

The electric field from an isolated positive charge

The electric field from an isolated negative charge

Field lines

Blow up a balloon, rub it against your head and then try to stick it to the wall. Write a brief report of why your investigation produced the result it did, using the ideas of electron transfer and static electricity.

1. What causes an object to become positively charged?
2. What happens when two objects with opposing charges are brought together?

Mind map

Potential difference

Series circuits

Parallel circuits

Work done

Power

Charge flow

Circuits

Energy transfers

Current

Static electricity

ELECTRICITY

Electric fields

Resistance

Resistors

ac current

dc current

Thermistors

LDR

Mains electricity

Filament bulb

Fuses

National Grid

Circuit breakers

Practice questions

1. Look at the parallel circuit below.

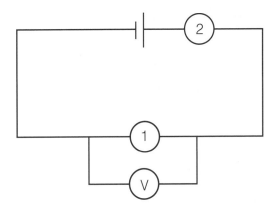

a) Component 1 has a resistance of 3 Ω and has a potential difference of 15 V across it. What is the current through it? **(3 marks)**

b) What is the current at point 2 in the circuit?
Explain how you arrived at your answer. **(2 marks)**

c) Sketch a graph to show the relationship between potential difference and current in an ohmic conductor. **(3 marks)**

d) Give an example of a component that would show a non-linear relationship between potential difference and current. **(1 mark)**

2. In an investigation into static electricity, a plastic rod was rubbed with a cloth. The rod was then used to pick up very small bits of paper.

a) After being rubbed with the cloth, the rod became positively charged. What can be deduced from the results of this investigation about the charge on the bits of paper? Explain your answer. **(2 marks)**

b) Use the concept of moving electrons to explain the change in charge of the rod during the investigation. **(2 marks)**

c) Explain what would happen if two identical rods that had been rubbed with the same type of cloth were brought close together. **(2 marks)**

Permanent and induced magnetism, magnetic forces and fields

Poles of a magnet

The poles of a magnet are the places where the magnetic forces are strongest. When two magnets are brought close together they exert a force on each other.

> Two like poles repel. Two unlike poles attract.

Attraction between opposite poles

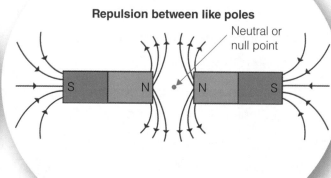

Repulsion between like poles

Neutral or null point

Magnetism is an example of a non-contact force.

Permanent magnetism vs induced magnetism

A **permanent magnet** . . .

➤ produces its own **magnetic field**.

An induced magnet . . .

➤ becomes a magnet when placed in a magnetic field
➤ always causes a force of attraction
➤ loses most or all of its magnetism quickly when removed from a magnetic field.

Magnetic field

The region around a magnet – where a force acts on another magnet or on a magnetic material (iron, steel, cobalt, magnadur and nickel) – is called the magnetic field.

A compass can be used to plot a magnetic field

The **force** between a magnet and a magnetic material is always attraction.

The **strength** of the magnetic field depends on the distance from the magnet.

The **field** is strongest at the poles of the magnet.

The **direction** of a magnetic field line is from the north pole of the magnet to the south pole of the magnet.

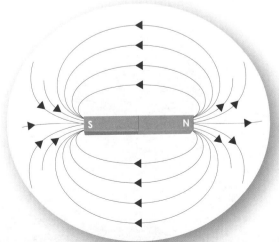

Compasses

A magnetic compass contains a bar magnet that points towards magnetic north. This provides evidence that the Earth's core is magnetic and produces a magnetic field.

Make your own compass using a bowl of water, a small dish, a magnet and a nail. To make a magnet for your compass, take the nail and magnet and stroke one end of the magnet along the length of the nail, always going in the same direction. Once your nail is magnetised, you need to float it in the water, then Start by putting a dish into the water, then place the nail into the centre of the dish. Let it settle a bit, to move around a little until it has found north.

1. What happens if the two north poles of a bar magnet are brought together?
2. When will a magnetic material become an induced magnet?
3. Where is the magnetic field of a magnet strongest?
4. Why does a magnetic compass point north?

Fleming's left-hand rule, electric motors and loudspeakers

Electromagnets

When a current flows through a conducting wire a magnetic field is produced around the wire.

The shape of the magnetic field can be seen as a series of concentric circles in a plane, perpendicular to the wire.

The direction of these field lines depends on the direction of the current.

The strength of the magnetic field depends on the current through the wire and the distance from the wire.

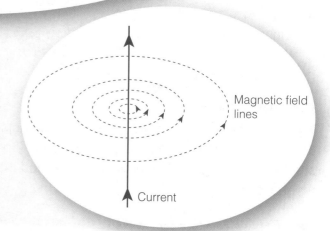

Magnetic field lines

Current

Coiling the wire into a **solenoid** (a helix) increases the strength of the magnetic field created by a current through the wire.

Features of a solenoid

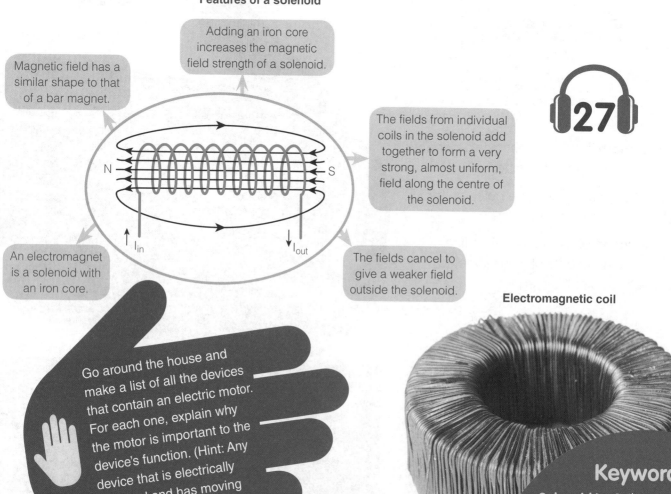

Adding an iron core increases the magnetic field strength of a solenoid.

Magnetic field has a similar shape to that of a bar magnet.

The fields from individual coils in the solenoid add together to form a very strong, almost uniform, field along the centre of the solenoid.

N   S

I_in   I_out

An electromagnet is a solenoid with an iron core.

The fields cancel to give a weaker field outside the solenoid.

Go around the house and make a list of all the devices that contain an electric motor. For each one, explain why the motor is important to the device's function. (Hint: Any device that is electrically powered and has moving parts will have a motor.)

27

Electromagnetic coil

Keyword

Solenoid ➤ Coil wound into a helix shape

Fleming's left-hand rule and the motor effect

When a conductor carrying a current is placed in a magnetic field, the magnet producing the field and the conductor exert an equal and opposite force on each other. This is the motor effect and is due to interactions between magnetic fields.

The direction of the force on the conductor can be identified using Fleming's left-hand rule.

If the direction of the current or the direction of the magnetic field is reversed, the direction of the force on the conductor is reversed.

The size of the force on the conductor depends on:
➤ the magnetic flux density
➤ the current in the conductor
➤ the length of conductor in the magnetic field.

For a conductor at right angles to a magnetic field and carrying a current, the force can be calculated using the following equation:

> **force = magnetic flux density × current × length**
>
> $F = BIl$
>
> ➤ force, F, in newtons, N
> ➤ magnetic flux density, B, in tesla, T
> ➤ current, I, in amperes, A (or amp)
> ➤ length, l, in metres, m

Example:
What is the force produced by a 0.5 m long conductor, with a magnetic flux of 1.2 T and a current of 16 A flowing through it?

$F = BIl$
$F = 1.2 \times 16 \times 0.5 = 9.6$ N

Electric motors

A coil of wire carrying a current in a magnetic field experiences a force, causing it to rotate. This is the basis of an **electric motor**.

The commutator and graphite brush allow the current to be reversed every half turn to keep the coil spinning.

Simple electric motor

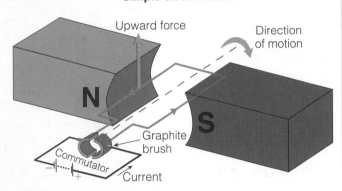

Loudspeakers and headphones

Loudspeakers and headphones use the motor effect to convert variations in current in electrical circuits to the pressure variations in sound waves.

1. What two things does the strength of a magnetic field around a wire depend on?
2. What shape is the magnetic field around a solenoid?
3. What three variables are related by Fleming's left-hand rule?

Induced potential and transformers

Keyword
Transformer ➤ Device used to increase or lower the voltage of an alternating current

🎧 **28**

The generator effect

A potential difference is induced across the ends of an electrical conductor when:
➤ the conductor moves relative to a magnetic field
➤ there is a change in the magnetic field around a conductor.

Induced current

When a potential difference is induced in a conductor that is part of a complete circuit, a current is induced.

The induced current generates a magnetic field. This magnetic field opposes the original change that generated the potential difference – either the movement of the conductor or the change in magnetic field.

The size of the induced potential difference, and therefore the induced current, can be increased by either:
➤ increasing the speed of movement
or
➤ increasing the strength of the magnetic field.

The direction of the induced potential difference and the induced current is reversed if either the direction of movement of the conductor is reversed or the polarity of the magnetic field is reversed.

🅦 Uses of the generator effect

The generator effect is used:
➤ In a dynamo to generate dc. A coil rotates inside the magnetic field of a permanent magnet, inducing a current in the coil. The current always flows in the same direction, producing the dc voltage-time graph below right.
➤ In an alternator to generate ac. A permanent magnet rotates inside a coil of wire, inducing the current in the coil. The current regularly reverses direction, producing the ac voltage-time graph below left.

ac current   **dc current**

Microphones use the generator effect to convert the pressure variations in sound waves into variations in current in electrical circuits.

1 Sound waves move the diaphragm backwards and forwards.

2 The diaphragm moves the coil backwards and forwards.

3 A changing current is induced in the coil that corresponds to the frequency of the sound.

4 This current is used to record the sound or it is fed into an amplifier and into a speaker to produce the sound.

Transformers

A basic **transformer** has a primary coil wire and a secondary coil of wire wound on an iron core. Iron is used as it is easily magnetised.

Iron core
Primary coil
Secondary coil

| An alternating current in the primary coil of a transformer produces a changing magnetic field in the iron core. | The changing magnetic field is also produced in the secondary coil. | An alternating potential difference is induced across the ends of the secondary coil. | An induced current will flow in the secondary coil if it is part of a complete circuit. |

The relationship between voltage and number of turns of the coil is given by the following equation:

$$\left[\frac{v_P}{v_S} = \frac{n_P}{n_S}\right]$$

➤ potential difference on primary and secondary coils, v_p and v_s in volts, V
➤ number of turns on the primary and secondary coil n_p and n_s

A step-up transformer has more turns on the secondary coil than the primary coil. A step-down transformer has more turns on the primary coil than the secondary coil.

In a step-up transformer, v_S is greater than v_P. In a step-down transformer, v_S is less than v_P.

The power output of a transformer relates to the power input and the potential difference in the coils.

$$V_s \times I_s = V_p \times I_p$$
➤ $V_s \times I_s$ is the power output (secondary coil)
➤ $V_p \times I_p$ is the power input (primary coil)
➤ power input and output, in watts, W

Example:
The power output required from a transformer is 500 W. The potential difference on the primary coil is 25 V. What current is required to produce this power output?

$$V_s \times I_s = V_p \times I_p$$
$$V_s \times I_s = 500 \text{ W} \quad \leftarrow \text{Required power output = 500 W}$$
$$500 \text{ W} = V_p \times I_p$$
$$500 \text{ W} = 25 \times I_p \quad \leftarrow V_p = 25 \text{ V}$$
$$\frac{500}{25} = I_p, \quad 20 \text{ A} = I_p$$

The equation linking potential difference and number of turns can be applied together with the equation for power transfer.

Example:
What number of turns on the secondary coil are required to produce a power output of 23 kW, if:
➤ the potential difference in the primary coil is 400 kV
➤ the primary coil has 26 000 turns
➤ the output current is 100 A?

$$V_s \times I_s = 23 \text{ kW}$$
$$100 \times V_s = 23 \text{ kW}$$
$$V_s = \frac{23}{100} = 0.23 \text{ kV}$$
$$\frac{N_p}{N_s} = \frac{400}{0.23} = 1739 \quad \leftarrow \left[\frac{v_p}{v_s} = \frac{n_p}{n_s}\right]$$
$$\frac{N_p}{N_s} = 1739$$
$$\frac{26000}{N_s} = 1739, \quad \frac{26000}{1739} = N_S$$
$$N_S = 15 \text{ turns} \quad \leftarrow \text{this is a step-down transformer}$$

By transmitting the power at high voltage through power cables, the current is kept low, reducing loss of heat energy. A step-down transformer can then be used to lower the voltage to a safer level.

Write down the stages of how a loudspeaker (see Module 27) and a microphone work. Mix them up and rearrange them to show how the sound of a voice is picked up by a microphone and then projected by a speaker.

1. Why is an iron core used in a transformer?
2. What type of current does a dynamo produce?
3. In what two ways can the induced current from a generator be increased?

Mind map

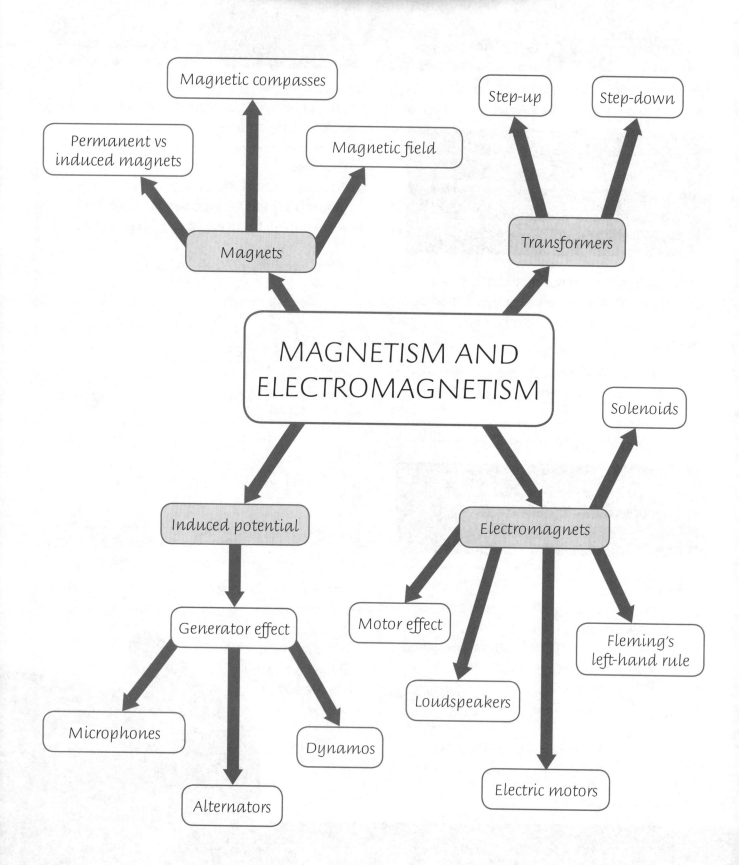

Magnetic compasses

Permanent vs induced magnets

Magnetic field

Magnets

Step-up

Step-down

Transformers

MAGNETISM AND ELECTROMAGNETISM

Solenoids

Induced potential

Electromagnets

Generator effect

Motor effect

Fleming's left-hand rule

Microphones

Loudspeakers

Dynamos

Alternators

Electric motors

Practice questions

1. The diagram below shows a bar magnet.

a) Draw the shape of the magnetic field around this magnet. **(2 marks)**

b) What would happen if the south pole of a bar magnet was brought into contact with the north pole of another magnet? **(1 mark)**

c) Give two differences between a bar magnet and an induced magnet. **(2 marks)**

2. The diagram shows a transformer.

Is this a step-up transformer or a step-down transformer?
How do you know? **(3 marks)**

3. Explain the importance of transformers to the National Grid. **(3 marks)**

4. If the transformer shown in the diagram had a potential difference of 15 V in its secondary coil, what would be the voltage in its primary coil? **(2 marks)**

Changes of state and the particle model

The particle model

Matter can exist as a solid, liquid or as a gas.

Solid – particles are very close together and vibrating. They are in fixed positions.

Liquid – particles are very close together but are free to move relative to each other. This allows liquids to flow.

Gas – particles in a gas are not close together. The particles move rapidly in all directions.

If the particles in a substance are more closely packed together, the density of the substance is higher. This means that liquids have a higher density than gases. Most solids have a higher density than liquids.

Density also increases when the particles are forced into a smaller volume.

Low density

High density

The density of a material is defined by the following equation:

$$\text{density} = \frac{\text{mass}}{\text{volume}}$$

$$\rho = \frac{m}{V}$$

➤ density, ρ, in kilograms per metre cubed, kg/m³
➤ mass, m, in kilograms, kg
➤ volume, V, in metres cubed, m³

Example:

What is the density of an object that has a mass of 56 kg and a volume of 0.5 m³?

$$\rho = \frac{m}{V}$$

$$= \frac{56}{0.5} = 112 \text{ kg/m}^3$$

When substances change state (melt, freeze, boil, evaporate, condense or sublimate), mass is conserved (it stays the same).

Changes of state are physical changes: the change does not produce a new substance, so if the change is reversed the substance recovers its original properties.

Ice

Water

Steam

29

Internal energy

Energy is stored inside a system by the particles (atoms and molecules) that make up the system. This is called **internal energy**.

Internal energy of a system is equal to the total kinetic energy and potential energy of all the atoms and molecules that make up the system.

Heating changes the energy stored within the system by increasing the energy of the particles that make up the system. This either raises the temperature of the system or produces a change of state.

Changes of heat and specific latent heat

When a change of state occurs, the stored internal energy changes, but the temperature remains constant. The graph below shows the change in temperature of water as it is heated; the temperature is constant when the water is changing state.

Heating curve for water

Keyword

Specific latent heat ➤ The energy required to change the state of one kilogram of the substance with no change in temperature

The **specific latent heat** of a substance is equal to the energy required to change the state of one kilogram of the substance with no change in temperature.

The energy required to cause a change of state can be calculated by the following equation:

$$\text{energy for a change of state} = \text{mass} \times \text{specific latent heat}$$

$$E = mL$$

➤ energy, E, in joules , J
➤ mass, m, in kilograms, kg
➤ specific latent heat, L, in joules per kilogram, J/kg

Example:

What is the energy needed for 600 g of water to melt? (The specific latent heat of water melting is 334 kJ/kg.)

$$E = mL$$
$$0.6 \times 334 = 200.4 \text{ kJ}$$

The specific latent heat of fusion is the energy required for a change of state from solid to liquid.

The specific latent heat of vapourisation is the energy required for a change of state from liquid to vapour

Time how long it takes a kettle to boil 0.5 litres, 1 litre and 1.5 litres of water. Use the concept of energy transfer to explain your results.

1. What energy is needed for 200 kg of iron to turn from a solid to a liquid? (The specific latent heat of iron melting is 126 kJ/kg.)
2. Explain the difference between the specific latent heat of fusion and the specific latent heat of vapourisation.
3. If a substance is heated but its temperature remains constant, what is happening to the substance?

Particle model and pressure

Keyword

Gas pressure ➤ Total force exerted by all of the gas molecules inside the container on a unit area of the wall

Gas under pressure

The molecules of a gas are in constant random motion.

When the molecules collide with the wall of their container they exert a force on the wall. The total force exerted by all of the molecules inside the container on a unit area of the wall is the **gas pressure**.

Increasing the temperature of a gas, held at constant volume, **increases** the pressure exerted by the gas.

Decreasing the temperature of a gas, held at constant volume, **decreases** the pressure exerted by the gas.

The temperature of the gas is related to the average kinetic energy of the molecules. The higher the temperature, the greater the average kinetic energy, and so the faster the average speed of the molecules. At higher temperatures, the particles collide with the walls of the container at a higher speed.

A gas can be compressed or expanded by pressure changes. The pressure produces a net force at right angles to the wall of the gas container (or any surface).

When the volume of the gas in the container is reduced, the pressure increases.

High pressure – Low volume

Low pressure – High volume

For a fixed mass of gas held at a constant temperature this equation is used:

constant = pressure × volume

constant = pV

➤ pressure, p, in pascals, Pa

➤ volume, V, in metres cubed, m^3

30

Draw a comic strip showing the effect of changing volume and temperature on a gas. Annotate your comic strip using the terms and equations in this module.

When a volume of a gas is altered, this allows the new pressure to be calculated by the following equation:

$$p_1 \times V_1 = p_2 \times V_2$$
- p_1 and V_2 are the initial pressure and volume
- p_1 and V_2 are the final pressure and volume

Example:

A gas with a pressure of 200 kPa is compressed from a volume of 3 m³ to a volume of 0.5 m³. What is the new pressure of the gas?

$$p_1 \times V_1 = p_2 \times V_2$$
$$200 \times 3 = p_2 \times 0.5$$
$$600 = p_2 \times 0.5$$
$$\frac{600}{0.5} = p_2$$
$$1200 \text{ kPa} = p_2$$

Doing work on a gas increases the internal energy of the gas and can cause an increase in the temperature of the gas. Look at this flow chart:

Pumping the handle of a bicycle pump is work done.

Energy is transferred to the air particles in the pump.

This increases the internal energy of the air particles.

As the particles in the air have more internal energy, the temperature of the air in the pump increases.

1. Explain how gases exert pressure.
2. When work is done to a gas, why does the temperature increase?

Mind map

Density

Pressure

Gas

Density

Liquids

Density

Solids

PARTICLE MODEL

Internal energy

Absolute zero

Specific latent heat

Specific latent heat of fusion

Specific latent heat of vapourisation

Practice questions

1. A solid has a mass of 150 g and a volume of 0.0001 m^3.

   a) What is the density of the solid? **(2 marks)**

   b) What happens to the mass and density of the solid when it sublimes? **(2 marks)**

   c) Explain what would happen to the stored internal energy and the temperature of the solid as it sublimed. **(2 marks)**

   d) The specific latent heat of the solid is 574 kJ/kg.

   What is the energy required for the solid to sublime? **(2 marks)**

2. a) Explain, using the particle model, why:

   i) a gas at a constant volume has a higher pressure when the temperature increases. **(2 marks)**

   ii) a gas at a constant temperature has a lower pressure when the volume increases. **(2 marks)**

   b) What is the new volume of a gas that changes its pressure from 500 kPa to 134 kPa? The initial volume was 2.1 m^3. **(3 marks)**

3. What term is given to the energy required for 1 kg of a liquid to become a gas? **(1 mark)**

Atoms and isotopes

Structure of atoms

Nucleus

(Not to scale)

Shell

Key: ● Proton ● Neutron ✕ Electron
(positive) (no change) (negative)

Atoms have a radius of around 1×10^{-10} metres.

The radius of a nucleus is less than $\dfrac{1}{10\ 000}$ of the radius of an atom.

Most of the mass of an atom is concentrated in the nucleus. Protons and neutrons have a relative mass of 1 while electrons have a relative mass of 0.0005. The electrons are arranged at different distances from the nucleus (are at different energy levels).

1st energy level   2nd energy level

Ca
20 P
20 N

4th energy level   3rd energy level

Absorption of electromagnetic radiation causes the electrons to become excited and move to a higher energy level and further from the nucleus.

Emission of electromagnetic radiation causes the electrons to move to a lower energy level and move closer to the nucleus.

If an atom loses or gains an electron, it is ionised.

The number of electrons is equal to the number of protons in the nucleus of an atom.

Atoms have no overall electrical charge.

All atoms of a particular element have the same number of protons. The number of protons in an atom of an element is called the **atomic number**.

The total number of protons and neutrons in an atom is called the **mass number**.

Mass number $\longrightarrow$ $^{4}_{2}\text{He}$ $\longleftarrow$ Element symbol
Atomic number $\longrightarrow$

Atoms of the same element can have different numbers of neutrons; these atoms are called isotopes of that element. For example, below are some isotopes of nitrogen. They each have 7 protons in the nucleus but different numbers of neutrons, giving the different isotopes.

$$^{14}\text{N} \quad ^{15}\text{N} \quad ^{13}\text{N}$$

Atoms turn into **positive ions** if they lose one or more outer electrons and into **negative ions** if they gain one or more outer electrons.

Write out the stages of the discovery of the atom on small cards. Mix them up then put them in the correct order.

The development of the atomic model

Before the discovery of the electron, atoms were thought to be tiny spheres that could not be divided.

The discovery of the electron led to further developments of the model. The plum pudding model suggested that the atom is a ball of positive charge with negative electrons embedded in it.

Spherical cloud of positive charge

Electron

Rutherford, Geiger and Marsden's alpha scattering experiment led to the conclusion that the mass of an atom was concentrated at the centre (nucleus) and that the nucleus was charged.

The nucleus

Orbits

Electrons

This evidence led to the nuclear model replacing the plum pudding model.

Niels Bohr suggested that the electrons orbit the nucleus at specific distances. The theoretical calculations of Bohr agreed with experimental observation.

Orbital electrons, negatively charged

Nucleus, containing positively charged protons

Later experiments led to the idea of the nucleus containing smaller particles with the same amount of positive charge (**protons**).

The experimental work of James Chadwick provided the evidence to show the existence of neutrons within the nucleus. This was about 20 years after the nucleus became an accepted scientific idea.

Keywords

Atomic number ➤ Number of protons in an atom

Mass number ➤ Total number of protons and neutrons in an atom

1. What is the effect on the electrons when an atom absorbs electromagnetic radiation?
2. What name is given to atoms of the same element that have different numbers of neutrons?
3. What is the difference between the plum pudding model and the nuclear model?

Radioactive decay, nuclear radiation and nuclear equations

Radioactive decay

Some atomic nuclei are unstable. The nucleus gives out radiation as it changes to become more stable. This is a random process called **radioactive decay**.

Activity is the rate at which a source of unstable nuclei decays, measured in **becquerel** (Bq).

➤ 1 becquerel = 1 decay per second

Count rate is the number of decays recorded each second by a detector, such as a Geiger-Müller tube.

➤ 1 becquerel = 1 count per second

Radioactive decay can release a neutron, alpha particles, beta particles or gamma rays. If radiation is ionising, it can damage materials and living cells.

Particle	Description	Penetration in air	Absorbed by...	Ionising power
Alpha particles (α)	Two neutrons and two protons (a helium nucleus).	a few centimetres	a thin sheet of paper	strongly ionising
Beta particles (β)	High speed electron ejected from the nucleus as a neutron turns into a proton.	a few metres	a sheet of aluminium about 5 mm thick	moderately ionising
Gamma rays (γ)	Electromagnetic radiation from the nucleus.	a large distance	a thick sheet of lead or several metres of concrete	weakly ionising

| Paper | 3–5 mm aluminium | Sheet of lead |

Strong ionising power α

Moderately ionising power β

Weak ionising power γ

Alpha is absorbed by a few centimetres of air or a thin sheet of paper.

Beta passes through air and paper but is absorbed by a few millimetres of aluminium.

Gamma is very penetrating and needs many centimetres of lead or many metres of concrete to absorb most of it.

Nuclear equations

Nuclear equations are used to represent radioactive decay.

Nuclear equations can use the following symbols:

$^{4}_{2}\textbf{He}$ alpha particle

$^{0}_{-1}\textbf{e}$ beta particle

Alpha decay causes both the mass and charge of the nucleus to decrease, as two protons and two neutrons are released.

$^{219}_{86}\textbf{radon} \rightarrow \ ^{215}_{84}\textbf{polonium} + \ ^{4}_{2}\textbf{He}$

Beta decay does not cause the mass of the nucleus to change but does cause the charge of the nucleus to increase, as a neutron becomes a proton.

$^{14}_{6}\textbf{carbon} \rightarrow \ ^{14}_{7}\textbf{nitrogen} + \ ^{0}_{-1}\textbf{e}$

The emission of a gamma ray does not cause the mass or the charge of the nucleus to change.

Alpha decay

Beta decay

Electron β−
Neutron
Proton

Make a large version of the radioactive decay table p. 80. Cut out each individual box to form separate cards. Mix the cards up and then group them to show the features of alpha, beta and gamma particles.

Make a large version of the radioactive decay table p. 80.

Keywords

Radioactive decay ➤ Random release of radiation from an unstable nucleus as it becomes more stable

Becquerel ➤ Unit of rate of radioactive decay

1. How far does alpha radiation penetrate in air?
2. What material is required to absorb gamma rays?
3. What effect does beta decay have on the mass and charge of the nucleus of an atom?

32

Half-lives and the random nature of radioactive decay

33

Uranium

Half-life

Radioactive decay occurs randomly. It is not possible to predict which nuclei will decay.

The half-life of a radioactive isotope is the time it takes for:

➤ the number of nuclei in a sample of the isotope to halve

or

➤ the count rate (or activity) from a sample containing the isotope to fall to half of its initial level.

For example:

A radioactive sample has an activity of 560 counts per second. After 8 days, the activity is 280 counts per second. This gives a half-life of 8 days.

The decay can be plotted on a graph and the half-life determined from the graph.

After 8 days, the counts per second had halved, therefore the half-life of this sample is 8 days

---

HT After another 8 days, the activity would now be 140 counts per second. As a ratio the total net decline is 140 : 560 or 1 : 4.

Radioactive contamination

Radioactive contamination is the unwanted presence of materials containing radioactive atoms or other materials.

This is a hazard due to the decay of the contaminating atoms. The level of the hazard depends on the type of radiation emitted.

Irradiation is the process of exposing an object to nuclear radiation. This is different from radioactive contamination as the irradiated object does not become radioactive.

Suitable precautions must be taken to protect against any hazard from the radioactive source used in the process of irradiation. In medical testing using radioactive sources, the doses patients receive are limited and medical staff wear protective equipment.

It is important for the findings of studies into the effects of radiation on humans to be published and shared with other scientists. This allows the findings of the studies to be checked by other scientists by the peer review process.

Shake ten or more coins in your hand and then drop them. Remove all the coins that are heads and record the number you've removed. Repeat the experiment until you have one or no coins left. Now plot a graph of how the number of coins in your hand decreased over time. Then, research graphs showing radioactive decay and compare them to the graph from your experiment.

1. Give the two definitions of half-life.
2. What is the half-life of a sample that goes from a count per second of 960 to 240 in 10 months?
3. Why is radioactive contamination a hazard?

Hazards and uses of radioactive emissions and background radiation

34

Background radiation

Background radiation is around us all the time.

Natural radiation sources	Man-made sources
Some rocks, such as granite.	Fallout from nuclear weapons testing.
Cosmic rays from space.	Fallout from nuclear accidents.

The level of background radiation and the radiation dose received by a person may be affected by their occupation and their location.

Radiation dose is measured in sieverts (Sv).
1000 millisieverts (mSv) = 1 sievert (Sv)

Cosmic Rays

Granite

Different half-lives of radioactive isotopes

Radioactive isotopes have a wide range of different half-life values.

Shortest half-lives	Longest half-lives
Unstable source	Stable source
Rapid decay	Slow decay
Large amount of radiation emitted in a short time	Small amount of radiation emitted per second but continues to emit radiation over a very long period of time
Example: lithium-4 has a half-life of 324×10^{-24}	Example: calcium-48 has a half-life of 43×10^{18} years

Radioactive isotopes with a long half-life can provide a long-term hazard because they continue to emit small amounts of radiation over a long period of time. Radioactive isotopes with a short half-life can provide a short-term danger as large amounts of radiation are released in a short time.

Keyword
Background radiation
➤ Radiation which is around us all the time

Uses of nuclear radiation

Nuclear radiations are used in medicine for:

➤ exploration of internal organs, such as the use of ^{13}N as a radioactive tracer
➤ control or destruction of unwanted tissue, e.g. gamma rays are used to destroy cancerous tumours.

A radiation source used as a tracer needs to have a long enough half-life to ensure it emits throughout the test period, but short enough that it doesn't continue to emit after the test period is over.

The radiation emitted should also be able to pass through body tissues so it can be detected but not cause any negative health effects for the patient or medical personnel.

As ionising radiation causes tissue damage, it is important to make sure that it is very well targeted when used to destroy cancer cells. Ionising radiation can also lead to mutations so it's important to balance this risk against the risk posed by the tumour to be destroyed.

Research the different uses of radiation in medicine and make a poster explaining the differences between the radiation used in tracers and the radiation used to kill cells.

1. Give one man-made source of background radiation and one natural source.
2. Is a highly unstable radioactive source likely to have a long or short half-life?
3. Give one use of nuclear radiation in medicine.

Nuclear fission and fusion

35

Keywords

Nuclear fission ➤ Splitting of a large and unstable atomic nucleus in a radioactive element

Nuclear fusion ➤ Joining of two light nuclei to form a heavier nucleus

Nuclear fission

Nuclear fission is the splitting of a large and unstable atomic nucleus in a radioactive element, such as uranium or plutonium. Spontaneous fission is rare.

Usually, for fission to occur the unstable nucleus must first absorb a neutron.

The nucleus splits into smaller nuclei.

When it splits, the nucleus emits two or three neutrons plus gamma rays.

Energy is released by the fission reaction.

The neutrons have kinetic energy and may go on to start a chain reaction.

In a nuclear reactor, the chain reaction is **controlled** to ensure the energy released can be controlled.

In a nuclear weapon, the chain reaction is **uncontrolled**, causing the energy to be released in an explosion.

Chain reaction

Neutron
Uranium nucleus

Neutron hits uranium nucleus

Uranium nucleus splits into smaller nuclei and some more neutrons

These neutrons hit more uranium nuclei

Nuclear fusion

Nuclear fusion is the joining of two light nuclei to form a heavier nucleus.

In this process some of the mass of the smaller nuclei is converted into energy of radiation.

Some of this energy may be the energy of emitted radiation.

Nuclei collide and fuse together

← Hydrogen-1

← Hydrogen-2

← Helium-3

Nuclear fusion occurs in stars

Write down each stage of nuclear fission and fusion on separate cards. Mix the cards up and then rearrange them to form the correct order for fission and fusion.

1. What may the neutrons released by nuclear fission cause?
2. Explain the difference between the release of energy in a nuclear reactor and from a nuclear weapon.

Mind map

Neutrons

Electrons

Natural

Man-made

Protons

Development of
the atomic model

Atoms

Background
radiation

ATOMIC STRUCTURE

Nuclear fission

Nuclear fusion

Radioactive decay

Half-life

Alpha particles

Radioactive
contamination

Beta particles

Gamma rays

Irradiation

Practice questions

1. The symbol below shows an element.

   $^{48}_{22}\text{Ti}$

   a) What is its . . .

      i) number of protons? **(1 mark)**

      ii) number of electrons? **(1 mark)**

      iii) number of neutrons? **(1 mark)**

   b) For parts **i)–iii)** above, explain how you arrived at your answers. **(6 marks)**

2. Experiments by Rutherford, Geiger and Marsden led to the plum pudding model being replaced by the nuclear model.

   a) Explain the differences between the plum pudding model and the nuclear model. **(2 marks)**

   b) How did the further work of Bohr and the further work of Chadwick refine the nuclear model? **(2 marks)**

3. The graph below shows the activity of a radioactive sample over time.

   a) What is the half-life of this sample?
      Explain how you arrived at your answer. **(2 marks)**

   b) Would this sample be useful as a radioactive tracer in medicine?
      Explain your answer. **(2 marks)**

Our solar system and the life cycle of a star

The planets in the **solar system** orbit the Sun (a **star**). Dwarf planets, such as Pluto, which also orbit the Sun and the natural satellites of planets (moons), are also part of the solar system.

NEPTUNE

URANUS

SATURN

JUPITER

MARS

EARTH

VENUS

MERCURY

Not to scale

The Sun

The Sun was formed from dust and gas (nebula) pulled together by gravitational attraction. Collisions between particles caused the temperature to increase enough for hydrogen nuclei to fuse together forming helium.

The energy released by nuclear fusion processes keeps the core of the Sun hot.

The Sun is stable. The force of gravity acting inwards and trying to collapse the Sun is in equilibrium (balanced) with the outward force produced by the fusion energy trying to expand the Sun.

The Sun is in the main sequence period of its life cycle.

The life cycle of a star

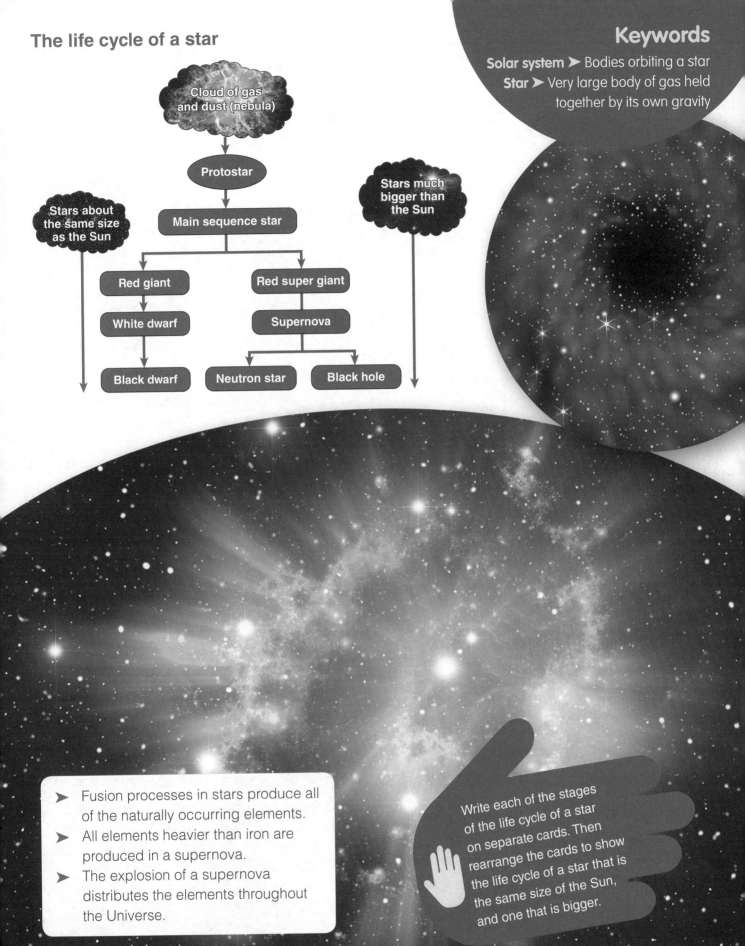

Cloud of gas and dust (nebula)

↓

Protostar

↓

Main sequence star

Stars about the same size as the Sun

Stars much bigger than the Sun

Red giant → White dwarf → Black dwarf

Red super giant → Supernova → Neutron star / Black hole

Keywords

Solar system ➤ Bodies orbiting a star
Star ➤ Very large body of gas held together by its own gravity

➤ Fusion processes in stars produce all of the naturally occurring elements.

➤ All elements heavier than iron are produced in a supernova.

➤ The explosion of a supernova distributes the elements throughout the Universe.

Write each of the stages of the life cycle of a star on separate cards. Then rearrange the cards to show the life cycle of a star that is the same size of the Sun, and one that is bigger.

1. What stage in its life cycle is the Sun currently in?
2. In a stable star, what force balances the fusion trying to expand the Sun?
3. What determines if a star forms a supernova or a white dwarf?
4. How are elements produced that are heavier than iron?

Orbital motion, natural and artificial satellites

Natural satellites

Planets orbit the Sun and a moon orbits a planet.

Sun

Earth

Moon

Not to scale

Man-made satellites

Artificial (man-made) **satellites** orbit the Earth and have a variety of functions including communication and weather monitoring.

Satellites in **geostationary orbits** always stay above the same point of the Earth. Satellites in **polar orbits** travel over both poles during an orbit. These orbits often only take a few hours.

Gravity provides the force that allows planets and satellites to maintain their circular orbits.

> **HT** For circular orbits, the force of gravity can lead to changing velocity but unchanged speed.
>
> If an object is in a stable orbit, the orbital radius must change if the object's speed changes.

Red shift

Our solar system is a small part of the **Milky Way** galaxy. There are hundreds of billions of other galaxies in the Universe.

Keywords

Satellite ➤ Object in orbit around a body
Gravity ➤ Process where all objects with mass attract each other

There is an observed increase in the wavelength of light from most distant galaxies. As the wavelength of visible light increases this leads to the light shifting to the red end of the spectrum. This effect is called **red-shift**.

Galaxies are moving away from the Earth. The further away the galaxies, the faster they are moving. Observations of supernovae suggest that distant galaxies are receding ever faster.

The faster movement leads to a larger observed increase in wavelength and so a larger red-shift.

WS This observed red-shift provides evidence that the universe is expanding and also supports the **Big Bang theory**. The Big Bang theory states that the universe began from a very small region that was extremely hot and dense. There is still much about the universe that is not understood, for example dark mass and dark energy.

Galaxy moving away

Wavelength

Faster moving galaxy

Wavelength increases

Using paper and string, construct a hanging mobile showing the Sun, Earth and Moon and their relative positions. You can extend this activity by adding in the other planets in the solar system.

1. Give two examples of uses of artificial satellites.
2. What happens to the speed and velocity of a moon as it orbits a planet?
3. What happens to the wavelength of light from a galaxy that is moving away from the Earth?
4. How does red-shift provide evidence for the Big Bang theory?

Mind map

Supernova

Natural

Artificial

Gravity

Life cycle of a star

Satellites

The Sun

SPACE PHYSICS

Planets in the solar system

Red shift

More distant galaxies moving away from Earth faster

Evidence for the Big Bang theory

Cosmic background radiation

Practice questions

1. a) Name two examples of natural satellites. **(1 mark)**

    b) Use the concept of balanced forces to explain why the Sun is currently stable. **(3 marks)**

    c) How will the final fate of the Sun differ from a star that has a much larger mass than the Sun? **(3 marks)**

2. a) The table below shows the changes in the observed wavelengths of light from three galaxies.

Galaxy	Change in wavelength
1	Increase
2	Decrease
3	Increase

    i)   Which of the galaxies' light is red-shifted? **(1 mark)**

    ii) Explain how you arrived at your answer to part **i)**. **(1 mark)**

    iii) What statement can be made about the movement of the galaxies whose light is red-shifted? **(1 mark)**

    iv) What theory of the beginning of the Universe does this help support? **(1 mark)**

    (b) Light from galaxies can also be blue-shifted.
    Explain what you think is meant by this term. **(3 marks)**

3. a) When a satellite is in a stable circular orbit, what statement can be made about the velocity of the satellite? **(1 mark)**

    b) What effect would a change in speed have on the orbital radius of a satellite? **(1 mark)**

Answers

Page 5

1. A scalar quantity only has a magnitude, a vector quantity has both a magnitude and a direction.
2. **Two from**: friction; air resistance; tension; normal contact force
3. $0.067 \times 10 = 0.67$ N
4. 78 J

Page 7

1. $0.1 \times 2 = 0.2$ N
2. Any point where the limit of proportionality hasn't been exceeded
3. Elastic potential energy

Page 9

1. The turning effect of a force
2. The total clockwise moment about the pivot equals the total anticlockwise moment about the pivot
3. $72 \times 0.7 = 50.4$ Nm

Page 11

1. $13 \times 1000 \times 10 = 130\,000$ Pa $= 130$ kPa
2. An object sinks because its weight is greater than the upthrust of the water
3. As the height of an object increases there are fewer air molecules above the object so their total weight is smaller.

Page 13

1. Distance has a magnitude but not a direction.
2. $\frac{10}{2.5} = 4$ km/h
3. Speed is a scalar quantity as it only has a magnitude. Velocity is speed in a given direction. Velocity has a magnitude and a direction so it is a vector quantity.

Page 15

1. Speed
2. A negative acceleration
3. The distance the object travels

Page 17

1. a) weight = mass × gravitational field strength
   $3.7 \times 187 = 691.9$ N **(2 marks)**
   b) Yes. The rover would weigh more (1870 N) **(1 mark)** as the gravitational field strength on Earth is greater than that on Mars **(1 mark)**
   c) pressure = height of the column × density of the liquid × gravitational field strength
   $= 3 \times 1000 \times 3.7 = 11.1$ kPa **(2 marks)**
2. a) i) Gradient of graph from 0–3 s $= \frac{25}{3} = 8.33$
      Acceleration $= 8.33$ m/s² **(2 marks)**
      ii) Area under graph 0–3 s $= 0.5 \times (3 \times 25) = 37.5$
      Distance travelled $= 37.5$ m **(2 marks)**
   b) Yes **(1 mark)** as the line on the graph is steeper from 0–3 than 3–6 / A steeper line indicates a faster acceleration **(1 mark)**

Page 19

1. 67 N
2. $89 \times 10 = 890$ N
3. It continues to move at the same speed.

Page 21

1. Thinking distance and braking distance
2. **Two from**: rain; ice; snow

Page 23

1. Airbags slow down a person's change in momentum in a collision.
2. $6 \times 4 = 24$ kg m/s
3. The momentum changes.

Page 25

1. a) The upward force from the ground is 890 N **(1 mark)** as it is equal and opposite to the force the cyclist is exerting on the ground **(1 mark)**.
   b) As the forces on the rider are balanced **(1 mark)** there is no resultant force and the rider would continue to move at a constant speed. This is Newton's first law **(1 mark)**.
   c) The backwards resultant force would be greater. **(1 mark)** so the rider would slow down **(1 mark)**.
2. a) resultant force = mass × acceleration
      $= 1200 \times 2.5 = 3000$ N or 3 kN **(2 marks)**
   b) momentum = mass × velocity
      $= 1200 \times 16 = 19\,200$ N kg m/s
   c) $F = \frac{m\,\Delta v}{\Delta t}$ **(1 mark)**
      momentum after crash = 0
      change in momentum = 19 200 **(1 mark)**
      force = 19 200 ÷ 0.4
      force = 48 000 N or 48 kN **(1 mark)**
   d) **Two from**: airbags; crumple zones; seatbelts **(2 marks)**

Page 27

1. $0.5 \times 0.065 \times 6^2 = 11.7$ J
2. $17 \times 987 \times 10 = 167.79$ kJ
3. It is the amount of energy required to raise the temperature of one kilogram of a substance by one degree Celsius.

Page 29

1. To ensure more energy is usefully transferred and less is wasted
2. $\frac{400}{652} = 0.61 = 61\%$
3. It reduces the thermal conductivity.

Page 31

1. Renewable. **Three from**: bio-fuel; wind; hydro-electricity; geothermal; tidal power; solar power; water waves
   Non-renewable. **Three from**: coal; oil; gas; nuclear fuel
2. The wind doesn't always blow and it's not always sunny, so electricity isn't always generated.
3. They produce carbon dioxide, which is a greenhouse gas. Increased greenhouse gas emissions are leading to climate change. Particulates and other pollutants are also released, which cause respiratory problems.

1. a) Renewable resources can be replenished as they are used **(1 mark)** whilst non-renewable energy resources will eventually run out **(1 mark)**
    b) Accidents at nuclear power stations could have devastating health and environmental effects **(1 mark)**. Nuclear waste is very hazardous **(1 mark)**.
    c) **Two from**: building tidal power stations involves the destruction of habitats; wind energy doesn't produce electricity all the time; some people think wind turbines are ugly and spoil the landscape **(2 marks)**
2. a) kinetic energy = 0.5 × mass × (speed)^2
        = 0.5 × 1600 × 32^2
        = 819 200 J or 819.2 kJ **(2 marks)**
    b) efficiency = $\frac{\text{useful output energy transfer}}{\text{useful input energy transfer}}$
        = $\frac{819.2}{1500}$ = 0.55 or 55% **(2 marks)**
    c) Sound **(1 mark)** and heat **(1 mark)**
    d) **One from**: lubrication; oil **(1 mark)**
3. a) g.p.e. = mass × gravitational field strength × height
        = 77 × 150 × 10
        = 115.5 kN **(2 marks)**
    b) kinetic energy = 0.5 × mass × (speed)^2
        = 0.5 × 77 × 20^2
        = 15.4 kN **(2 marks)**
    c) Gravitational potential energy to kinetic energy **(1 mark)** to elastic potential energy **(1 mark)**

Waves

Page 35

1. Longitudinal: Sound wave
    Transverse: **One from**: water wave; electromagnetic wave
2. The distance from a point on one wave to the equivalent point on an adjacent wave
3. It will increase

Page 37

1. The angle of reflection
2. Ear drum
3. 20 Hz to 20 kHz

Page 39

1. P-waves are longitudinal and travel at different speeds through solids and liquids. S-waves are transverse and cannot travel through a liquid.
2. Similarity: Both use reflection of waves.
    Difference: In ultrasound, waves are partially reflected when they meet a boundary between two different media. In echo sound, waves are reflected off the seafloor or solid objects in the water.
3   They cannot travel through the liquid outer core of the Earth.

Page 41

1. Infrared radiation
2. Visible light
3. Towards the normal

Page 43

1. By oscillations in electrical circuits
2. Mutation of genes and cancer
3. **One from**: energy efficient lamps; sun tanning

Page 45

1. A virtual image
2. Blue
3. 4.25 cm

Page 47

1. It absorbs all of the radiation incident on it, it does not reflect or transmit any radiation and it is the best possible emitter as it emits the maximum amount of radiation possible at a given temperature.

2. **Two from**: the rate of absorption of radiation; the rate of emission of radiation; the rate of reflection of radiation into space
3. Its temperature will remain constant

Page 49

1. Compression is a region in a longitudinal wave where the particles are closer together **(1 mark)**. Rarefaction is a region in a longitudinal wave where the particles are further apart **(1 mark)**
2. frequency = $\frac{\text{wave speed}}{\text{wavelength}}$
        = $\frac{200}{3.2}$
        = 62.5 Hz **(2 marks)**
3. P-waves travel through solids and liquids **(1 mark)** whereas S-waves cannot travel through a liquid **(1 mark)**. Only P-waves are detected on the opposite side of the Earth from the epicentre of the earthquake, not S-waves **(1 mark)** therefore the outer core of the Earth is liquid **(1 mark)**.
4. original height = $\frac{\text{image height}}{\text{magnification}}$
        = $\frac{5}{2.2}$
        = 2.3 cm **(2 marks)**
5. a) Convex lens **(1 mark)**
    b)

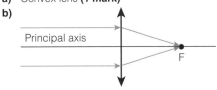

Principal axis

F

(1 mark)

6. Green plants reflect green light so appear green **(1 mark)** whilst all other colours of light are absorbed by the plant **(1 mark)**.

7. Sound travels as a **longitudinal** wave. When a sound wave travels in air the oscillations of the air particles are **parallel** to the direction of energy transfer. The sound wave **doesn't transfer matter, only energy**. **(3 marks)**

8. High frequency sound (sonar) is produced by the fishing boat **(1 mark)**. The high frequency sound is reflected off the shoal of fish and the reflection is detected by the boat **(1 mark)**. The difference in time between the ultrasound being produced and the reflection being detected allows the distance to the fish shoal to be determined **(1 mark)**.

Electricity

Page 51

1. The symbol for a variable resistor has an arrow through it.
2. 4.2 C
3. 90 A

Page 53

1. Because resistance depends on light intensity
2. An ammeter and a voltmeter
3. 8 V
4. 2 Ω

Page 55

1. 5 A
2. Add the resistances of both resistors together
3. Lower

Page 57

1. Blue.
2. The earth wire is a safety wire to stop the appliance becoming live.
3. Touching a live wire would produce a large potential difference across the body.

Page 59

1. $5^2 \times 2 = 50$ W
2. $60 \times 12 = 720$ J
3. They lower the potential difference of the transmission cables to a safe level for domestic use.

Page 61

1. The loss of electrons
2. They will attract

Page 63

1. a) $\text{current} = \dfrac{\text{potential difference}}{\text{resistance}}$

   $= \dfrac{15}{3}$

   $= 5$ A **(3 marks)**

   b) 5 A **(1 mark)**. The current is the same at all points in a series circuit **(1 mark)**.

   c)

   (3 marks)

   d) **One from**: filament lamp; LDR; diode; thermistor **(1 mark)**

2. a) The bits of paper were either uncharged or negatively charged **(1 mark)** because they were attracted to the positively charged rod **(1 mark)**.

   b) Electrons were transferred from the rod to the cloth **(1 mark)**. The loss of electrons meant the rod had a positive charge **(1 mark)**.

   c) They would repel **(1 mark)** as they have the same charge (positive) **(1 mark)**.

Magnetism and Electromagnetism

Page 65

1. They would repel
2. When it's placed in a magnetic field
3. At the poles of the magnet
4. The Earth's core is magnetic and produces a magnetic field.

Page 67

1. The current through the wire and the distance from the wire
2. The same shape as the magnetic field around a bar magnet
3. Magnetic field, force and current

Page 69

1. It is easily magnetised
2. direct current
3. By increasing the speed of movement or increasing the strength of the magnetic field

Page 71

1. a)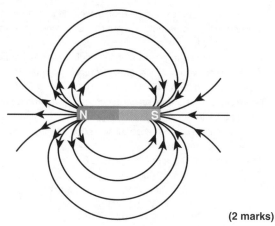

   (2 marks)

   b) The magnets would attract **(1 mark)**.

   c) An induced magnet is only magnetic when placed in a magnetic field whilst a bar magnet is always magnetic **or** An induced magnet always causes a force of attraction while a bar magnet can cause a force of attraction or repulsion. **(2 marks)**

2. It is a step-down transformer **(1 mark)** as there are fewer coils on the secondary coil than on the primary coil **(1 mark)**. A step-up transformer would have more coils on the secondary coil than the primary coil **(1 mark)**.

3. Step-up transformers increase voltage for transmission in high voltage cables **(1 mark)**. The current is kept low, reducing loss of heat energy **(1 mark)**. A step-down transformer lowers the voltage to a safer level for use in houses **(1 mark)**.

4. $\dfrac{\text{number of turns on primary coil}}{\text{number of turns on secondary coil}} = \dfrac{6}{2} = 3$ **(1 mark)**

   $3 = \dfrac{\text{potential difference on primary coil}}{\text{potential difference on secondary coil}}$

   $3 = \dfrac{\text{potential difference on primary coil}}{15\text{ V}}$

   $3 \times 15 = \text{potential difference on primary coil}$

   potential difference on primary coil = 45 V **(1 mark)**

Particle Model of Matter

Page 73

1. $200 \times 126 = 25\,200$ kJ
2. Specific latent heat of fusion is the energy required for a change of state from solid to liquid. Specific latent heat of vapourisation is the energy required for a change of state from liquid to vapour.
3. It is changing state.

Page 75

1. When the molecules collide with the wall of their container they exert a force on the wall, causing pressure.
2. The internal energy of the gas increases.

Page 77

1. a) $\text{density} = \dfrac{\text{mass}}{\text{volume}}$

   $= \dfrac{0.15}{0.0001}$

   $= 1500$ kg/m^3 **(2 marks)**

   b) The mass remains constant **(1 mark)** and the density decreases **(1 mark)**.

   c) The temperature would remain constant as it was changing state **(1 mark)** and the solid's internal energy would increase **(1 mark)**.

   d) energy for a change of state = mass × specific latent heat

   $= 0.15 \times 574\,000$

   $= 86.1$ kJ or 86100 J **(2 marks)**

2. **a)** **i)** The particles gain kinetic energy as the temperature increases **(1 mark)**. This increases the speed at which the particles collide with the sides of the container they are in **(1 mark)**.

ii) The same number of particles occupy a greater volume **(1 mark)**, reducing the rate of collisions with the sides of the container **(1 mark)**.

b)
$$p_1 \times V_1 = p_2 \times V_2$$
$$500 \times 2.1 = 134 \times V_2 \textbf{ (1 mark)}$$
$$\frac{(500 \times 2.1)}{134} = V_2 \textbf{ (1 mark)}$$
$$V_2 = 7.8 \text{ m}^3 \textbf{ (1 mark)}$$

3. Specific latent heat of vaporisation **(1 mark)**

Atomic Structure

Page 79

1. The electrons become excited and move to a higher energy level, further from the nucleus.

2. Isotopes

3. The plum pudding model suggested the atom was a ball of positive charge with negative electrons embedded in it. The nuclear model has a nucleus with electrons orbiting.

Page 81

1. A few centimetres

2. **Accept any dense material**, e.g.: concrete or lead.

3. The mass of the nucleus doesn't change but the charge of the nucleus does change.

Page 83

1. When the time taken for the number of nuclei in a sample of the isotope halves, or when the count rate (or activity) from a sample containing the isotope falls to half of its initial level.

2. 5 months

3. The radioactive atoms decay and release radiation.

Page 85

1. Man-made source. **One from**: fallout from nuclear weapons testing; fallout from nuclear accidents
Natural source. **One from**: some rocks (such as granite); cosmic rays from space

2. A short half-life

3. **One from**: killing cells (such as cancer); exploring internal organs (such as tracers)

Page 87

1. Further fission or a chain reaction

2. The energy release from a nuclear reactor is controlled.
The energy release from a nuclear weapon is uncontrolled.

Page 89

1. **a)** **i)** 22 **(1 mark)**
ii) 22 **(1 mark)**
iii) 26 **(1 mark)**

b) **i)** Number of protons is the atomic number **(1 mark)**, which is the bottom number on the symbol **(1 mark)**.

ii) The number of electrons equals the number of protons **(1 mark)**. The number of protons is 28 **(1 mark)**.

iii) The number of neutrons is the mass number **(1 mark)**. The number of protons is 48 – 22 = 26 **(1 mark)**.

2. **a)** The plum pudding model suggested that the atom is a ball of positive charge with negative electrons embedded in it **(1 mark)**. Rutherford, Geiger and Marsden said the mass of an atom was concentrated in the nucleus with electrons orbiting the nucleus **(1 mark)**.

b) Niels Bohr suggested that the electrons orbit the nucleus at specific distances **(1 mark)**. Chadwick provided the evidence for the existence of the neutron within the nucleus **(1 mark)**.

3. **a)** 60 days **(1 mark)**. This is the point where the counts per second have halved (Also accept $\frac{800}{2}$ = 400) **(1 mark)**

b) No **(1 mark)** because its half-life is too long so it would persist in the body for too long **(1 mark)**.

Space Physics

Page 91

1. Main sequence

2. The force of gravity

3. Its mass

4. In a supernova

Page 93

1. **Two from**: weather monitoring; spying; communications

2. The speed remains constant. The velocity constantly changes.

3. The wavelength increases and is shifted to the red end of the spectrum.

4. Galaxies are moving away from the Earth. The further away the galaxies, the faster they are moving.

Page 95

1. **a)** **Two from**: moons; planets; comets **(1 mark)**

b) The outward force from nuclear fusion **(1 mark)** is balanced by **(1 mark)** the force of gravity **(1 mark)**.

c) The Sun will become a black dwarf **(1 mark)**. A larger star would become a neutron star or a black hole **(1 mark)** and would supernova while our Sun wouldn't **(1 mark)**.

2. **a)** **i)** Galaxies 1 and 3 **(1 mark)**
ii) These wavelengths increase so the light is moving towards the red end of the spectrum **(1 mark)**.
iii) These galaxies are moving away from Earth **(1 mark)**.
iv) The Big Bang theory **(1 mark)**

b) The wavelength of light decreases **(1 mark)** so is shifted towards the blue end of the spectrum **(1 mark)** so the galaxies are moving towards Earth **(1 mark)**.

3. **a)** The velocity is constantly changing **(1 mark)**.

b) A change in speed would cause the orbital radius to change **(1 mark)**.

Physics Equations

force = mass × acceleration

kinetic energy = 0.5 × mass × (speed)^2

momentum = mass × velocity

work done = force × distance (along the line of action of the force)

$$\text{power} = \frac{\text{work done}}{\text{time}}$$

$$\text{efficiency} = \frac{\text{useful output energy transfer}}{\text{useful input energy transfer}}$$

gravity force = mass × gravity constant (g)

potential energy = mass × height × gravitational constant (g) in a gravitational field

force exerted by a spring = extension × spring constant

moment of a force = force × distance (normal to direction of the force)

distance travelled = speed × time

$$\text{acceleration} = \frac{\text{change in velocity}}{\text{time}}$$

wave speed = frequency × wavelength

charge flow = current × time

potential difference = current × resistance

power = potential difference × current = (current)^2 × resistance

energy transferred = power × time = charge flow × potential difference

Physics Equations

$$\text{density} = \frac{\text{mass}}{\text{volume}}$$

$$\text{pressure} = \frac{\text{force normal to a surface}}{\text{area of that surface}}$$

$$(\text{final velocity})^2 - (\text{initial velocity})^2 = 2 \times \text{acceleration} \times \text{distance}$$

change in thermal energy = $m \times$ specific heat capacity $\times$ change in temperature

thermal energy for a change of state = $m \times$ specific latent heat

energy transferred in stretching = $0.5 \times$ spring constant $\times (\text{extension})^2$

$$\begin{aligned}\text{potential difference across primary coil} \\ \times \text{ current in primary coil}\end{aligned} = \begin{aligned}\text{potential difference across secondary coil} \\ \times \text{ current in secondary coil}\end{aligned}$$

pressure $\times$ volume = constant (for a given mass of gas and at a constant temperature) for gases

---

HT force on a conductor (at right angles to a magnetic field) carrying a current $=$ magnetic flux density $\times$ current $\times$ length

$$\frac{\text{potential difference across primary coil}}{\text{potential difference across secondary coil}} = \frac{\text{number of turns in primary coil}}{\text{number of turns in secondary coil}}$$

pressure due to a column of liquid = height of column $\times$ density of liquid $\times g$

The Periodic Table

Key

■ Metals
■ Non-metals

Key element box:
- Relative atomic mass → 1
- Atomic symbol → **H**
- Name → hydrogen
- Atomic number → 1

Group 1	2											3	4	5	6	7	0 or 8
																	4 **He** helium 2
7 **Li** lithium 3	9 **Be** beryllium 4											11 **B** boron 5	12 **C** carbon 6	14 **N** nitrogen 7	16 **O** oxygen 8	19 **F** fluorine 9	20 **Ne** neon 10
23 **Na** sodium 11	24 **Mg** magnesium 12											27 **Al** aluminium 13	28 **Si** silicon 14	31 **P** phosphorus 15	32 **S** sulfur 16	35.5 **Cl** chlorine 17	40 **Ar** argon 18
39 **K** potassium 19	40 **Ca** calcium 20	45 **Sc** scandium 21	48 **Ti** titanium 22	51 **V** vanadium 23	52 **Cr** chromium 24	55 **Mn** manganese 25	56 **Fe** iron 26	59 **Co** cobalt 27	59 **Ni** nickel 28	63.5 **Cu** copper 29	65 **Zn** zinc 30	70 **Ga** gallium 31	73 **Ge** germanium 32	75 **As** arsenic 33	79 **Se** selenium 34	80 **Br** bromine 35	84 **Kr** krypton 36
85 **Rb** rubidium 37	88 **Sr** strontium 38	89 **Y** yttrium 39	91 **Zr** zirconium 40	93 **Nb** niobium 41	96 **Mo** molybdenum 42	[98] **Tc** technetium 43	101 **Ru** ruthenium 44	103 **Rh** rhodium 45	106 **Pd** palladium 46	108 **Ag** silver 47	112 **Cd** cadmium 48	115 **In** indium 49	119 **Sn** tin 50	122 **Sb** antimony 51	128 **Te** tellurium 52	127 **I** iodine 53	131 **Xe** xenon 54
133 **Cs** caesium 55	137 **Ba** barium 56	139 **La*** lanthanum 57	178 **Hf** hafnium 72	181 **Ta** tantalum 73	184 **W** tungsten 74	186 **Re** rhenium 75	190 **Os** osmium 76	192 **Ir** iridium 77	195 **Pt** platinum 78	197 **Au** gold 79	201 **Hg** mercury 80	204 **Tl** thallium 81	207 **Pb** lead 82	209 **Bi** bismuth 83	[209] **Po** polonium 84	[210] **At** astatine 85	[222] **Rn** radon 86
[223] **Fr** francium 87	[226] **Ra** radium 88	[227] **Ac*** actinium 89	[261] **Rf** rutherfordium 104	[262] **Db** dubnium 105	[266] **Sg** seaborgium 106	[264] **Bh** bohrium 107	[277] **Hs** hassium 108	[268] **Mt** meitnerium 109	[271] **Ds** darmstadtium 110	[272] **Rg** roentgenium 111							

Elements with atomic numbers 112–116 have been reported but not fully authenticated.

*The lanthanoids (atomic numbers 58–71) and the actinoids (atomic numbers 90–103) have been omitted.

The relative atomic masses of copper and chlorine have not been rounded to the nearest whole number.

Notes

Notes

GCSE Success

AQA

Physics

Exam Practice Workbook

Complete Revision & Practice

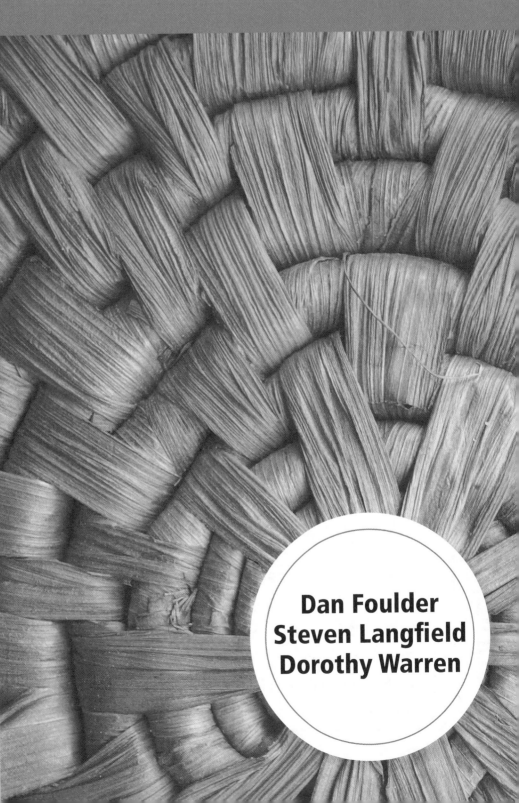

Dan Foulder
Steven Langfield
Dorothy Warren

Physics

Contents

1 Neil, an astronaut, has a mass of 78 kg.

(a) Calculate Neil's weight.

(gravitational field strength = 10 N/kg) (1)

....

(b) The Moon has a gravitational field strength of 1.6 N/kg.

What would Neil's mass and weight be on the Moon? (2)

....

....

(c) Neil also has a gravitational field that causes attraction.

Explain why this has no measurable effect on either the Moon or the Earth. (2)

....

....

2 The diagram shows Louise, a runner.

(a) Calculate the resultant force acting on Louise. (2)

....

....

(b) The forces on Louise changed as shown by the diagram below.

(i) What is the resultant force on Louise now? (1)

....

(ii) What statement can be made about her speed now? Explain your answer. (2)

....

....

(c) Louise uses 90 N of force and the work done is 25 kJ. What distance does she cover? (2)

....

....

For more help on this topic, see Letts GCSE Physics Revision Guide pages 4–5

1 The graph below shows the results of an extension of a spring in response to different forces.

(a) What term is given to the relationship shown in this graph? (1)

....

(b) Calculate the spring constant for this spring. (3)

....

....

....

(c) The results were repeated, but with a larger range of masses providing the force. The results are shown in the graph below.

(i) What term is given to the relationship shown in this graph? (1)

....

(ii) Explain the difference in the shapes of the two graphs. (3)

....

....

....

For more help on this topic, see Letts GCSE Physics Revision Guide pages 6–7

1 Calculate the force applied on the spanner in the diagram. (3)

17 cm

25 N

....

....

....

....

2 The diagram below shows a see-saw being used by two people.

Person B

Person A

1.5 m

x m

360 N

Pivot
(fulcrum)

500 N

At what distance is person A sitting to balance the see-saw? Explain how you arrived at your answer. (3)

....

....

....

3 The diagram below shows three gears.

Gear A turns anticlockwise.

A

B

C

(a) Add arrows to the diagram to show the direction of movement of gears B and C. (2)

(b) Which statement is true? Tick **one** box. (1)

Gear B will rotate slower than gear A. ☐

Gear B will rotate faster than gear A. ☐

Gears B and A will rotate at the same speed. ☐

For more help on this topic, see Letts GCSE Physics Revision Guide pages 8–9

1 A fluid exerts a pressure over an area of 0.6 m^2.

The force exerted is 500 N.

(a) What pressure is exerted by the fluid? (2)

....

....

HT **(b)** The fluid is in a column. The fluid has a density of 1100 kg/m^3 and the gravitational field strength is 10 N/kg. How high is the column of fluid? (2)

....

....

HT **2** Anna carried out an investigation into floating a boat on fresh water. On each attempt, the boat she made sank.

(a) Explain, using the concept of unbalanced forces, why the boat sank. (3)

....

....

....

(b) Suggest and explain an improvement Anna could make to increase the chances of the boat floating. (3)

....

....

....

(c) Fresh water has a density of 1000 kg/m^3. Seawater has a density of 1029 kg/m^3. Anna predicts that the boat is more likely to float on seawater than on fresh water. Evaluate her prediction. (3)

....

....

....

....

Pressure in a fluid

Module 4

For more help on this topic, see Letts GCSE Physics Revision Guide pages 10–11

1 **(a)** Explain why speed is a scalar quantity while velocity is a vector quantity. (2)

....

....

HT **(b)** Why does a car travelling around a bend at a constant speed have a constantly
changing velocity? (2)

....

....

(c) Draw lines to match the following average speeds to the methods of travel. (4)

Average speed	**Travel method**
1.5 m/s	Car
6 m/s	Plane
20 m/s	Bicycle
250 m/s	Walking

2 **(a)** A jet ski travels 180 metres in 13 seconds. What is its speed? (2)

....

....

(b) How long would it take for the same jet ski travelling at the same speed to travel 500 m? (2)

....

....

For more help on this topic, see Letts GCSE Physics Revision Guide pages 12–13

1 The graph shows the distance a boat travels over time.

(a) What is the average speed of the boat over the first 350 seconds? (2)

....

....

....

....

(b) What is the velocity of the boat at 265 seconds? (2)

....

....

2 The graph shows the velocity of a car.

(a) (i) During what time period is the greatest acceleration of the car? (1)

....

....

(ii) What is the acceleration during this time period? (2)

....

....

HT **(b)** How far did the car travel in 0–50 seconds? (3)

....

....

3 Explain why a skydiver in free fall accelerates for a time before maintaining a

constant speed. .... (4)

....

....

....

Distance–time and velocity–time graphs

Module 6

1 **(a)** What will happen if a resultant force greater than zero is applied to:

    (i) a stationary object? (1)

    ....

    (ii) a moving object? (1)

    ....

(b) Which of Newton's laws deals with the effect of resultant force? (1)

....

HT **(c)** What term is given to the tendency of objects to continue in their state of rest? (1)

....

2 **(a)** The acceleration of an object is inversely proportional to the mass of an object. How does the acceleration relate to the resultant force? (1)

....

(b) (i) Adele, a cyclist, who has a total mass of 110 kg, accelerates at 5 m/s^2. What is the resultant force on Adele? (2)

    ....

    ....

    (ii) Explain how the resultant force on Adele will change as she slows down and comes to a stop. (3)

    ....

    ....

    ....

3 State Newton's third law. (1)

....

4 Use Newton's laws to explain the events that the sign below is warning about. (3)

....

....

....

....

**Weak bridge
$\frac{1}{4}$ mile
ahead**

17^T

For more help on this topic, see Letts GCSE Physics Revision Guide pages 18–19

1 The graph below shows the effect on stopping distance of a wet road compared to a dry road.

(a) Does the wet road affect the thinking distance or the braking distance of the car? Explain your answer. (2)

....

....

(b) Explain the difference in the results between the wet road and the dry road. (3)

....

....

....

(c) Increasing speed increases the thinking distance and the braking distance of a car. Explain why. (2)

(i) Thinking distance: ....

....

(ii) Braking distance: ....

....

(d) Give **two** other factors that could increase the thinking distance. (2)

....

....

For more help on this topic, see Letts GCSE Physics Revision Guide pages 20–21

Forces and braking

Module 8

HT **1** **(a)** What is the momentum of a 50 kg cheetah running at 20 m/s? (2)

....

....

(b) What will happen to the cheetah's momentum as it decelerates? (1)

....

HT **2** **(a)** **(i)** A car is travelling at 13 m/s when it crashes into a wall. Charlie, the driver, with a mass of 90 kg, is wearing a seatbelt and comes to rest in 0.12 seconds. What is the force produced by the change in Charlie's momentum? (3)

....

....

....

(ii) If Charlie had not been wearing a seatbelt, he would have come to rest in 0.01 seconds. Calculate the rate of change in momentum of Charlie in this situation. (2)

....

....

(iii) Use the two values for rate of change of momentum to evaluate the effectiveness of the seatbelt. (2)

....

....

(iv) Identify **two** other safety features which reduce the rate of change of momentum. (2)

....

....

For more help on this topic, see Letts GCSE Physics Revision Guide pages 22–23

1 Jessica, a sky diver, is in a plane at a height of 3900 m. She has a mass of 60 kg.

(a) What is Jessica's gravitational potential energy?

(Assume gravitational field strength is 10 N/kg.) (2)

....

....

(b) Jessica jumps from the plane and accelerates to a terminal velocity of 55 m/s.
What is Jessica's kinetic energy at this point? (2)

....

....

(c) Jessica deploys her parachute and slows to a speed of 5 m/s.
What is her new kinetic energy? (2)

....

....

(d) When Jessica lands on the ground, she is stationary. What is her kinetic energy now? (1)

....

2 The table below shows the specific heat capacity of different substances.

Substance	Specific heat capacity J/kg/°C
Water	4180
Copper	390
Ethanol	2440
Titanium	520

(a) Which substance would require the least energy to raise 1 kg by 1°C?
Explain how you arrived at your answer. (2)

....

....

(b) Calculate the mass of copper that requires 76 kJ of energy to increase in temperature
from 16°C to 35°C. (3)

....

....

....

For more help on this topic, see Letts GCSE Physics Revision Guide pages 26–27

Changes in energy

Module 10

1 Which of the below is an incorrect ending to the following sentence?
Tick the correct options. (2)

Energy cannot be…

created. ☐

transferred. ☐

destroyed. ☐

dissipated. ☐

2 The table below shows the average cost of heating three different houses.
Each home is the same size.

House	Heating cost per hour / p
A	105
B	88
C	150

(a) Which house is likely to have the best insulation in its walls?
Explain how you arrived at your answer. (3)

....

....

....

(b) Can you be certain about your conclusion?
Explain your answer. (3)

....

....

....

(c) The boiler in another house is 65% efficient. If the energy input is 5400 kJ,
what is the useful energy output? (2)

....

....

For more help on this topic, see Letts GCSE Physics Revision Guide pages 28–29

1 Complete the table below to give **three** examples of renewable energy and **three** examples of non-renewable energy. (3)

Renewable energy	Non-renewable energy

2 The graph below shows the percentage of the total electricity in the UK generated by wind turbines.

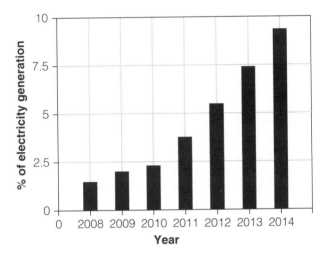

(a) Describe the trend shown by the graph. (1)

....

(b) Describe the main advantage of wind power over burning fossil fuels. (2)

....

....

(c) Will wind turbines ever make up 100% of electricity generation? Explain your answer. (3)

....

....

....

(d) Why might some people not want wind turbines to be placed on the tops of hills? (1)

....

For more help on this topic, see Letts GCSE Physics Revision Guide pages 30–31

1 The speed of sound in water is 1482 m/s.

(a) What type of wave is a sound wave when travelling in air? (1)

....

(b) Calculate the wavelength of a sound wave in water that has a frequency of 120 Hz. (2)

....

....

(c) Explain what would happen to this sound's wavelength when it passes from water into air. (2)

....

....

(d) The speed of sound in air is 330 m/s.
Suggest a reason for the difference between this speed and the speed of sound in water. (2)

....

....

(e) How do the oscillations in a water wave differ to the oscillations in a sound wave travelling in air? (2)

....

....

2 Draw lines to match the following terms to their correct definitions. (3)

Amplitude	The distance from a point on one wave to the equivalent point on the adjacent wave.
Wavelength	The number of waves passing a point each second.
Frequency	The maximum displacement of a point on a wave away from its undisturbed position.

For more help on this topic, see Letts GCSE Physics Revision Guide pages 34–35

1 The diagram below shows the reflection of a beam of light.

(a) Label angles **A** and **B**. (2)

(b) Determine the value of angle **A**. (2)

....

....

HT **2** The graph below shows the hearing ranges of different organisms.

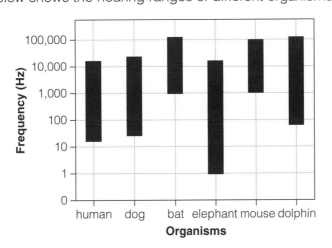

(a) Which of the organisms can hear ultrasound? (2)

....

....

(b) Not all humans can hear the full range of frequencies shown in the graph above.
Give two reasons why. (2)

....

....

For more help on this topic, see Letts GCSE Physics Revision Guide pages 36–37

Module 14

HT ❶ The diagram below shows the waves produced by an earthquake.

Epicentre

B

A

Crust

Mantle

Outer core

Inner core

(a) Identify waves **A** and **B**. (2)

A: ....

B: ....

(b) Explain how the diagram above provides evidence that the Earth has a liquid outer core. (3)

....

....

....

HT ❷ The diagram below shows a scan of a foetus.

Explain how ultrasound was used to produce this image. (3)

....

....

....

....

For more help on this topic, see Letts GCSE Physics Revision Guide pages 38–39

1 The image below shows the electromagnetic spectrum.

Wavelength (metres)	A	Microwave	B	Visible	Ultraviolet	X-ray	C
	10^3	10^{-2}	10^{-5}	10^{-6}	10^{-8}	10^{-10}	10^{-12}

What are the names of the different types of electromagnetic radiation **A**–**C**? (3)

A: ....

B: ....

C: ....

HT **2** The diagram shows the effect of light entering water from the air.

(a) Give the names of angles **A** and **B**. (2)

A: ....

B: ....

(b) Explain why the light changes direction as it moves from air to water. (3)

....

....

....

(c) How would refraction differ if the light was entering air from water? (1)

....

For more help on this topic, see Letts GCSE Physics Revision Guide pages 40–41

Electromagnetic waves and properties 2

HT **1** Draw lines to match up the following types of radiation to their uses and why they are suitable for that use.

(3)

Radiation type	Use	Why suitable for use?
Radio waves	Heating a room	Don't require a direct line of sight between transmitter and receiver.
Ultraviolet	Television	Require less energy than conventional lights.
Infrared	Energy efficient lamps	Thermal radiation heats up objects.

2 **(a)** From where do gamma rays originate? (1)

....

(b) Why are gamma rays potentially harmful? (2)

....

....

3 What variable could be measured to determine the possible harm caused by radiation? (1)

....

HT **4** This photograph shows a medical image.

(a) What type of electromagnetic radiation is used to produce this image? (1)

....

(b) Explain why this type of radiation is used in medical imaging. (3)

....

....

....

For more help on this topic, see Letts GCSE Physics Revision Guide pages 42–43

1 The diagram below shows light through a lens.

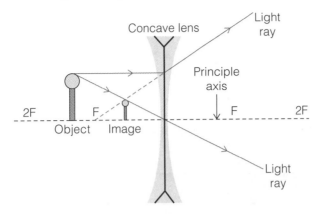

Identify the type of lens. (1)

....

2 The diagram below shows what happens when light hits a material.

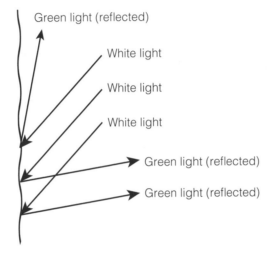

(a) Is this material **opaque**, **transparent** or **translucent**? (1)

....

(b) What type of reflection is shown in this diagram? (1)

....

(c) What colour could the material be? Explain your answer. (2)

....

....

For more help on this topic, see Letts GCSE Physics Revision Guide pages 44–45

1 What are the **three** characteristics of a perfect black body? (3)

....

....

....

HT **2** In an investigation into the effects of heating on a metal, the following three stages occurred.

Stage	Description
A	The metal was heated and its temperature rose.
B	The metal began to glow white hot and the temperature of the metal was constant.
C	The heating was stopped and the metal began to cool.

(a) Explain the events at stages **A**–**C** in terms of absorption and emission of energy. (5)

A: ....

....

B: ....

....

C: ....

....

HT **3** Between 1880 and 1920 the Earth's average temperature ranged from 13.6 °C to 13.9 °C.

(a) What statement can be made about the absorption and emission of radiation by the Earth during this period? (1)

....

....

(b) An increase in man-made carbon dioxide levels is causing more thermal energy to be absorbed by the atmosphere rather than being radiated back into space.

Explain the effect of this on Earth's mean temperature. (2)

....

....

For more help on this topic, see Letts GCSE Physics Revision Guide pages 46–47

1 Identify the following circuit symbols:

(a) (1)

....

(b) (1)

....

(c) (1)

....

2 The diagram shows a circuit.

(a) Identify components **X**, **Y** and **Z**. (3)

X: ....

Y: ....

Z: ....

(b) Ammeter **1** gave a reading of 5 amps.
What is the reading of ammeter **2**? (1)

....

(c) What is 'electric current'? (1)

....

(d) If the charge flow through the circuit was 780 C, for how long was the current
flowing through the circuit? (2)

....

....

For more help on this topic, see Letts GCSE Physics Revision Guide pages 50–51

1 The graph shows the relationship between the current and potential difference of a component.

Current

Potential difference

(a) What general name could be given to this type of conductor? (1)

....

(b) What environmental factor could change and lead to a change in the shape of the graph above?

(1)

....

(c) On the axis, sketch a graph to show the relationship between current and potential difference through a diode. (2)

Current

Potential difference

2 Calculate the current flowing through a 4 Ω resistor when there is a potential difference of 15 V across it.

(2)

....

....

3 Look at the circuit below.

Explain why this circuit could not be used to determine the resistance of the bulb. (3)

....

....

....

For more help on this topic, see Letts GCSE Physics Revision Guide pages 52–53

1 The diagram shows a circuit.

(a) What type of circuit is shown? (1)

....

....

4 Ω   5 Ω   2 Ω

(b) What is the total resistance of the three resistors
in the circuit? Show how you arrived at your answer. (2)

....

....

2 The diagram shows a circuit.

(a) What is the current at **1**? (1)

....

....

(b) What is the voltage at **2**? (1)

....

....

(c) What is the resistance at **3**? (1)

....

....

8 V

A 4 A

A 2 A   **3**

A **1**   ⊗

V **2**

(d) The circuit was rewired so that the lamp and resistor were wired in series. How would
this change the total resistance of the two components?

Explain your answer. (3)

....

....

....

For more help on this topic, see Letts GCSE Physics Revision Guide pages 54–55

Series and parallel circuits

Module 22

1 Draw lines to match the names of the wires in a plug to its colour and function. (3)

Wire	Colour	Function
Live wire	Blue	Completes the circuit.
Neutral wire	Brown	Only carries a current if there is a fault.
Earth wire	Green and yellow stripes	Carries the alternating potential difference from the supply.

2 An electric sander is being used during a house renovation. The sander is plugged into a socket in the wall.

(a) Is the sander powered by direct current or alternating current? Explain your answer. (2)

....

....

....

(b) Fully explain why it would be dangerous to operate the sander if the wire became damaged. (4)

....

....

....

....

(c) Explain why this risk would be decreased if the sander was powered by two 1.5V batteries. (2)

....

....

For more help on this topic, see Letts GCSE Physics Revision Guide pages 56–57

1 (a) A tumble dryer has a current flowing through it of 3 A and a resistance of 76.7 Ω.

Calculate its power. (2)

....

....

(b) What useful energy transfers are occurring in the tumble dryer? (2)

....

....

(c) If the tumble dryer transfers 180 kJ of energy in a cycle, how long is the cycle
in seconds? (2)

....

....

(d) The mains electricity used by the tumble dryer has a potential difference of 230 V.
Some of the overhead cables that carry the electricity in the National Grid have a
potential difference of 138 kV.

Explain the reasons for this difference in potential difference. (3)

....

....

....

For more help on this topic, see Letts GCSE Physics Revision Guide pages 58–59

1 When two insulators are rubbed together they may become electrically charged.

(a) Why is this described as static electricity? (1)

....

(b) What causes the build-up of static charge? (2)

....

....

2 In an investigation into static electricity, two charged objects were brought towards each other and experienced a force. The closer the objects, the greater the force pushing them away from each other.

Use the concept of electrical fields to explain the results of this investigation. (3)

....

....

....

3 The diagrams below show the electrical fields around two charged objects.

Which of the charged objects would have the strongest electrical field?

Explain your answer.

A   B   (3)

....

....

....

For more help on this topic, see Letts GCSE Physics Revision Guide pages 60–61

1 Complete the diagram below to show the poles of the three bar magnets interacting. (3)

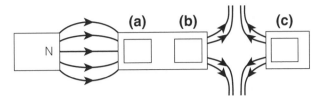

2 The diagram below shows an experiment into magnets and magnetic objects.

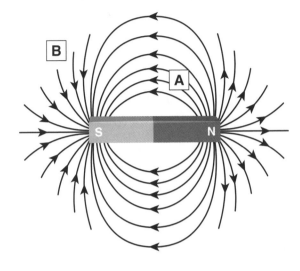

(a) What name is given to the region around the magnet where magnetic objects or magnets experience a force? (1)

....

(b) What type of force would a magnetic object placed at **A** experience? (1)

....

(c) Would the force at **A** be stronger than the force experienced by a magnetic object at **B**? Explain your answer. (2)

....

....

3 The bar magnet in a compass points towards magnetic north. What can be concluded about the Earth's core from this fact? (3)

....

....

....

1 Tick each of the following statements that correctly describe the features of a solenoid. (2)

The magnetic field around a solenoid is the same shape as the magnetic field around a bar magnet. ☐

Adding an iron core to a solenoid reduces the magnetic strength of the solenoid. ☐

A solenoid with an iron core is an electromagnet. ☐

A solenoid with a tin core is an electromagnet ☐

A solenoid is a non-conducting wire formed into a helix. ☐

HT **2** A conducting wire is placed in a magnetic field. When a current is passed through the wire it begins to move.

(a) What **two** things could be altered to cause the wire to move in the opposite direction? (2)

....

....

(b) What name is given to this effect? (1)

....

(c) The wire is at a right angle to the magnetic field. The wire is 30 cm long and has a current of 15 A flowing through. This produces 25 N of force.

What is the magnetic flux density? (2)

....

....

HT **3** Explain how the motor effect can be used to produce sound using a loudspeaker. (4)

....

....

....

....

....

....

....

....

For more help on this topic, see Letts GCSE Physics Revision Guide pages 66–67

HT **1** Explain how a microphone uses the generator effect to convert pressure variations in sound waves to variations in an electric current. (4)

....

....

....

....

HT **2** (a) Identify the **two** types of current shown by the graphs below. (2)

A

B

....

(b) Explain how an alternator is used to generate current **B**. (3)

....

....

....

HT **3** The diagram below shows a transformer.

Primary   Secondary

V_P V_S

Soft iron core

(a) Why is iron used as the core of an electromagnet? (1)

....

(b) What would be the output voltage of the transformer if the input voltage was 400 V? (3)

....

....

....

For more help on this topic, see Letts GCSE Physics Revision Guide pages 68–69

1 (a) A full fire extinguisher has a mass of 5 kg and a volume of 0.002 m³.
What is the density of a fire extinguisher? (2)

....

....

(b) What would happen to the density of the fire extinguisher after it had been used to
put out a fire? Explain your answer. (3)

....

....

....

2 The graph below shows the results of an investigation into the heating of a substance.

(a) At what temperatures did the substance do the following?

(i) Melt: .... (1)

(ii) Boil: .... (1)

(b) Explain how you arrived at your answers for part **(a)**. (3)

....

....

....

(c) The substance has a specific latent heat of melting of 250 kJ/kg. What is the energy
required to melt 500 g of the substance? (2)

....

....

For more help on this topic, see Letts GCSE Physics Revision Guide pages 72–73

1 In an investigation into the link between pressure and molar concentration of a gas, the temperature and volume are kept constant.

(a) Explain the importance of controlling the following variables.

(i) Constant temperature (1)

....

(ii) Constant volume (1)

....

(b) A gas used in a different experiment had a pressure 10 kPa in a volume of 0.6 m³. The gas was then compressed into a volume of 0.2 m³ at the end of the experiment. What is the new pressure of the gas? (3)

....

....

....

2 Mike is using a helium tank to fill a birthday balloon. The balloon inflates but then pops.

(a) Use the concept of gas pressure to explain these events. (3)

....

....

....

....

....

(b) Mike suggested that the balloon popped as the room was too cold. Explain why this explanation is unlikely to be correct. (2)

....

....

....

....

For more help on this topic, see Letts GCSE Physics Revision Guide pages 74–75

Particle model and pressure

Module 30

1 An element symbol is shown below.

(a) State the numbers of the following subatomic particles that an atom of the element contains.

(i) Protons: .... (1)

(ii) Neutrons: .... (1)

(iii) Electrons: .... (1)

(b) The element is also found in the following forms:

^{12}C ^{13}C ^{14}C

(i) What name is given to these forms? (1)

....

(ii) How do they differ from each another? (1)

....

2 (a) Give **two** differences between the plum pudding model of atomic structure and Rutherford, Geiger and Marsden's nuclear model. (2)

....

....

(b) Why was James Chadwick's experimental work in 1932 important in further developing the model of atomic structure? (1)

....

For more help on this topic, see Letts GCSE Physics Revision Guide pages 78–79

1 An investigation was carried out into the penetration of radiation emitted from different radioactive sources.

Type of radiation	Radiation released	Penetration distance in air
A	Two neutrons and two protons (a helium nucleus).	A few centimetres.
B	Electromagnetic radiation from the nucleus.	A large distance.
C	High speed electron ejected from the nucleus as a neutron turns into a proton.	A few metres.

(a) (i) Identify the types of radiation **A–C**. (3)

A: ....

B: ....

C: ....

(ii) Rank the radiations in **(i)** from most ionising to least ionising. (2)

....

Most ionising   **Least ionising**

2 The equation below shows the decay of a radioactive element.

$$^{238}_{A}U \longrightarrow ^{B}_{90}Th + ^{C}_{D}\alpha$$

(a) What type of decay is shown by the equation? (1)

....

(b) Complete the missing parts (**A–D**) of the equation. (3)

A: ....

B: ....

C: ....

D: ....

(c) What effect does gamma emission have on the nucleus of a radioactive element? (1)

....

....

For more help on this topic, see Letts GCSE Physics Revision Guide pages 80–81

Radioactive decay and nuclear radiation and nuclear equations

Module 32

1 Complete the following paragraph using some of the words below. (3)

| decay | irradiation | Sievert | contamination |
| radioactive | half-life | emit | radiation |

Radioactive .... is the unwanted presence of materials containing

radioactive atoms on other materials. This is a hazard due to the .... of

the contaminating atoms. The atoms will .... radiation so may be a hazard.

.... is the process of exposing an object to nuclear ....

without the object itself becoming ....

2 The graph below shows the decay of a radioactive element.

(a) (i) Estimate the half-life of this element. (1)

....

(ii) Explain how you arrived at your answer. (1)

....

(iii) Estimate the counts per second of the sample after 60 days. (2)

....

....

For more help on this topic, see Letts GCSE Physics Revision Guide pages 82–83

1 Match the sources of radiation below to the following categories in the table. Write your answers in the table. (2)

Granite

Cosmic rays from space

Fallout from nuclear accidents

Fallout from nuclear weapons testing

Natural radiation sources	Man-made sources

2 Explain the difference in the hazards posed by short half-life radioactive isotopes compared to long half-life radioactive isotopes. (4)

....

....

....

3 Explain how and why the nuclear radiation used to destroy unwanted tissues is different from the radiation used in the exploration of internal organs. (4)

....

....

....

....

For more help on this topic, see Letts GCSE Physics Revision Guide pages 84–85

1 The diagram below shows a nuclear reaction.

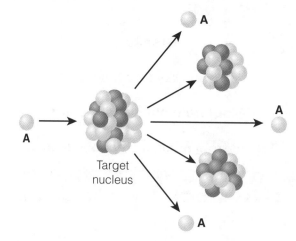

Target nucleus

(a) (i) What type of reaction is shown in the diagram? (1)

....

(ii) What are the **A** particles? (1)

....

(b) Explain how the energy released in the reaction differs in a nuclear reactor compared to in a nuclear weapon. (2)

....

....

....

2 The equation below shows an example of nuclear fusion.

$$^{2}_{1}\text{H} + ^{3}_{1}\text{H} \longrightarrow ^{4}_{2}\text{He} + ^{1}_{0}\text{n}$$

Explain fully what the equation shows and why energy is released. (3)

....

....

....

For more help on this topic, see Letts GCSE Physics Revision Guide pages 86–87

1 (a) Place the numbers **1–5** next to the following statements to give the correct order of events that occur during the life cycle of a star. (3)

Supernova ☐

Main sequence star ☐

Protostar ☐

Red super giant ☐

Neutron star ☐

(b) What statement can be made about the mass of the star in this flow chart compared to the mass of our Sun?
Explain your answer. (3)

....

....

....

2 (a) Draw lines to match the following elements to when they were produced. (2)

He •

Ti •

N •

Pb •

• Produced during star's main sequence

• Produced in a supernova

(b) Explain why you matched the elements as you did in part **(a)**. (2)

....

....

....

(c) What process produces elements during the main sequence of a star? (1)

....

For more help on this topic, see Letts GCSE Physics Revision Guide pages 90–91

1 (a) Give **two** examples of natural satellites that orbit the Sun. (2)

....

....

HT (b) How do the following variables change in a stable orbit of a moon? (2)

Speed:..

Velocity: ....

2 Read the following extract and use it to answer the question below.

In the static universe theory *it is believed that the Universe is a finite size and is not expanding or contracting. It is also believed that the Universe has existed and will continue to exist infinitely. An early proposer of the theory was Giordano Bruno in 1584.*

This theory is no longer considered correct.

Explain why the 'static universe theory' is considered incorrect, giving evidence that supports the current Big Bang theory. (4)

....

....

....

....

....

....

....

....

....

For more help on this topic, see Letts GCSE Physics Revision Guide pages 92–93

GCSE
PHYSICS
Higher Tier Paper 1H

Time allowed: 1 hour 45 minutes

You may use:

- a ruler
- a calculator
- the Physics Equation Sheet.

Instructions

- Answer all questions in the spaces provided.
- Do all rough work in this book. Cross through any work you do not want to be marked.

Information

- There are 100 marks available on this paper.
- The marks for questions are shown in brackets.
- You are expected to use a calculator where appropriate.
- You are reminded of the need for good English and clear presentation in your answers.
- When answering question 10.4 you need to make sure that your answer:

  - is clear, logical, sensibly structured
  - fully meets the requirements of the question

Advice

- In all calculations, show clearly how you work out your answer.

Name: _____

This question is about circuits.

| 0 | 1 |.| 1 | Which of the following circuit diagram symbols represents a thermistor?
Tick (✓) **one** box.

[1 mark]

| 0 | 1 |.| 2 | The diagrams below show four circuits. Each circuit has two **identical** bulbs connected in parallel.

In which circuit will the ammeters have the same reading?
Tick (✓) **one** box.

[1 mark]

| 0 | 1 |.| 3 | A torch bulb has a resistance of 1200 Ω. The bulb operates when the current through it is 0.005 A.
How many 1.5 V batteries will the torch need to operate? [3 marks]

_____

_____

_____

0 1 . 4 Alex and Louise want to find out the identity of the mystery electrical component contained in Box Z. They connect it in the circuit shown in **Figure 1**.

Figure 1

They change the potential difference, measure the current and plot the results (see **Figure 2**).

Figure 2

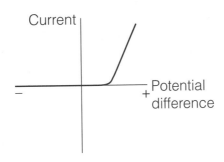

Write down the name of the mystery component in Box Z.
Explain your answer using ideas about resistance. **[3 marks]**

_____

_____

_____

0 2 This question is about isotopes of carbon.

0 2 . 1 Complete **Table 1** to show the atomic structures of the three isotopes of carbon. **[3 marks]**

Table 1

Isotope	Number of protons	Number of neutrons	Number of electrons
Carbon-12	6	6	6
Carbon-13			
Carbon-14			

0 2 . 2 Carbon-14 is an unstable isotope. It undergoes beta decay to form nitrogen-14.

Describe what happens in the nucleus of an atom to form a beta particle. **[2 marks]**

_____

_____

| 0 | 2 | . | 3 | The half-life for the decay of carbon-14 is 5730 years.

Explain what is meant by the term half-life. **[1 mark]**

_____

_____

| 0 | 2 | . | 4 | The very small amount of carbon-14 in a plant remains constant until the plant dies. The amount of carbon-14 then falls steadily as the plant decays. The amount of carbon-12 stays the same.

The plant material can be dated by measuring the ratio of carbon-14 to carbon-12.

Complete **Table 2**. **[1 mark]**

Table 2

Number of half-lives	Time after death of organism in years	$^{14}C : {}^{12}C$ ratio/10^{-12}
0	0	1.000
1	5730	0.500
2	11 460	0.250
3	_____	0.125

| 0 | 2 | . | 5 | Use the data from **Table 2** to plot a decay curve for carbon-14 (see **Figure 3**). **[2 marks]**

Figure 3

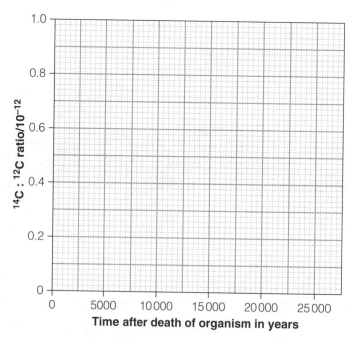

| 0 | 2 | . | 6 | A sample of wood taken from an old shipwreck had a carbon-14 : carbon-12 ratio/10^{-12} of 0.3.

Use **Figure 3** to estimate the age of the wood. **[1 mark]**

_____

| 0 | 3 | This question is about electrical appliances.

| 0 | 3 | . | 1 | Look at **Figure 4**. Which set of conditions would you find on the label of a microwave oven that operates with the mains electricity supply in the UK?
Tick (✓) **one** box.

[1 mark]

Figure 4

50 Hz, 230 V, ac ☐

50 Hz, 230 V, dc ☐

60 Hz, 230 V, dc ☐

60 Hz, 230 V, ac ☐

| 0 | 3 | . | 2 | **Figure 5** shows a symbol found on hairdryers.

Figure 5

☐

The symbol shows that the hairdryer is double insulated. What does this mean?
Tick (✓) **one** box.

[1 mark]

It has a moulded plastic plug. ☐

It does not need an earth wire. ☐

The case has metal parts on the outside. ☐

The dryer has double plastic coating on the wires. ☐

| 0 | 3 | . | 3 | Look at the diagram of a three-pin plug in **Figure 6**.

Figure 6

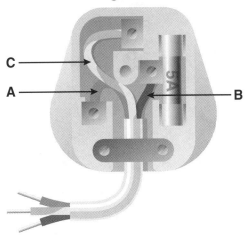

Complete **Table 3**.

[2 marks]

Wire	Name	Colour
A	_____	Blue
B	Live	_____
C	_____	Green and yellow stripes

| 0 | 3 | . | 4 | Give **three** reasons why wire C in **Figure 6** is connected to some domestic appliances. **[3 marks]**

_____

_____

_____

| 0 | 3 | . | 5 | The plug in **Figure 6** is connected to an electric drill and contains a 5 A fuse.

Explain how a fuse protects the user. **[4 marks]**

_____

_____

_____

_____

| 0 | 3 | . | 6 | The electric drill has a power rating of 960 W.

Calculate the value of the current passing through the fuse when the drill is operating normally at 230 V. Show all your working. Give your answer to two significant figures. **[3 marks]**

_____

_____

_____

Answer: _____ A

| 0 | 4 | Look at the picture of the roller coaster in **Figure 7**.

Figure 7

0 4 . 1 At what position have the roller coaster cars got maximum kinetic energy?
Tick (✓) **one** box.   **[1 mark]**

Position 1 ☐

Position 2 ☐

Position 3 ☐

Position 4 ☐

0 4 . 2 Describe the energy changes that take place as the roller coaster cars travel from position 1 to position 4.   **[2 marks]**

_____

_____

_____

0 4 . 3 Explain why the next 'hill' on the roller coaster after position 4 has to be lower than position 1.   **[3 marks]**

_____

_____

_____

0 5 **Figure 8** shows an electric screwdriver. This question is about motors used in electric screwdrivers.

Figure 8

0 5 . 1 Complete **Table 4**.   **[1 mark]**

Table 4

Electric motor	Input electrical power (W)	Useful output power (W)	Wasted power (W)
A	209	220	11
B	172	160	12
C	235	223	12
D	205	193	12
E	242	_____	20

0 5 . 2 Name the motor with the largest useful power output. _____ **[1 mark]**

0 5 . 3 Describe how the electrical power is used and suggest how some power is wasted. **[2 marks]**

_____

_____

_____

0 5 . 4 Calculate the efficiency of electric motor B. **[2 marks]**

_____

_____

_____

0 6 This question is about energy, work done and power.

0 6 . 1 Which of the following vehicles has the greatest kinetic energy?
Tick (✓) **one** box.

[1 mark]

A van with a mass of 1500 kg travelling at 11 m/s ☐

A car with a mass of 1400 kg travelling at 12 m/s ☐

A van with a mass of 1200 kg travelling at 12 m/s ☐

A car with a mass of 1100 kg travelling at 13 m/s ☐

0 6 . 2 **Figure 9** shows an electric motor lifting a load.

Figure 9

How much work (in joules) is done when the load is lifted through a height of 2.5 m?
Show all your working. **[2 marks]**

_____

_____

0 6 . 3 It takes four seconds to lift the load through 2.5 m. Calculate the power of the motor. Show all your working. **[2 marks]**

_____

_____

0 7 **Figure 10** shows some meteorites that Mahri is investigating.

Figure 10

0 7 . 1 Draw a labelled diagram to describe how she can measure the volume of each meteorite. **[2 marks]**

0 7 . 2 Mahri measures the volume of each meteorite three times. How does this improve her results? **[2 marks]**

_____

_____

0 7 . 3 What other measurement does Mahri need to take so that she can calculate the density of the meteorites? **[1 mark]**

_____

0 7 . 4 **Table 5** shows the densities of common elements found in meteorites.

Table 5

Element	Density kg/m³
Aluminium	2712
Iron	7850
Magnesium	1738
Nickel	8908
Silicon	2328

The mean density of the three meteorites was 7965 kg/m³. Analysis indicated that two elements were present. Iron formed 90% of the composition. What was the element making up the remaining 10%?

Tick (✓) **one** box.

[1 mark]

Aluminium ☐

Magnesium ☐

Nickel ☐

Silicon ☐

| 0 | 8 | Look at **Table 6**, which shows the specific heat capacity of four metals.

Table 6

Metal	Aluminium	Copper	Iron	Lead
Specific heat capacity J/kg °C	900	490	390	130

| 0 | 8 | . | 1 | If you were given a 2 kg block of each metal, which metal would take the least amount of energy to raise its temperature from 20°C to 25°C?

Tick (✓) **one** box.

[1 mark]

Aluminium ☐

Copper ☐

Iron ☐

Lead ☐

| 0 | 8 | . | 2 | As shown in **Figure 11**, a 500 g block of copper was heated with a 100 W electric immersion heater for 85 seconds.

Figure 11

Calculate the amount of energy in joules supplied to the copper block. Show all your working.

[2 marks]

_____

_____

_____

0 8 . 3 In a repeat experiment, the copper block started at a temperature of 22°C and was supplied with 9065 J of energy. What was its final temperature? Show all your working. **[3 marks]**

change in thermal energy = mass × specific heat capacity × temperature change

0 8 . 4 The specific heat capacity of ice is 2108 J/kg°C. The latent heat of ice is 334000 J/kg.

Explain why these numbers are different. **[3 marks]**

0 8 . 5 A well-insulated beaker contains 200 g of water at 20°C. This will release 16800 J of energy to cool down to 0°C.

60 g of ice at 0°C is added to the water.

If no heat energy is lost or gained by the beaker, will all of the ice melt?
Explain your answer. **[3 marks]**

energy for a change of state = mass × specific latent heat

specific latent heat of fusion of water = 334000 J/kg

0 9 This question is about nuclear fission and fusion.

0 9 . 1 Uranium-238 decays by emitting an alpha particle.

Complete the equation by writing the atomic number and mass number for thorium in the boxes. **[2 marks]**

$$^{238}_{92}U \longrightarrow \boxed{}_{\boxed{}}Th + {}^{4}_{2}He$$

0 9 . 2 Modern nuclear power stations use the energy from the fission of uranium atoms to generate electricity. A chain reaction starts when a neutron is fired into a uranium-235 nucleus.

Explain how the chain reaction continues once started. **[3 marks]**

_____

_____

_____

0 9 . 3 Boron rods are used in a nuclear core to control the reaction.

Describe how the boron control rods prevent the chain reaction from getting out of control.

[2 marks]

_____

_____

0 9 . 4 Nuclear fusion could be a major energy source for the future. Extreme conditions are required to carry out a fusion reaction.

What extreme conditions are used? Explain why they are required. **[3 marks]**

_____

_____

_____

0 9 . 5 The electrical output of a power station is connected to transformers (see **Figure 12**).

Figure 12

The output from the transformers is connected to the National Grid.

Describe the role of the transformers and how they benefit the transmission of electricity.

[3 marks]

_____

_____

_____

0 9 . 6 The UK government has proposed that new nuclear power stations should be built.

Outline **one** advantage and **one** disadvantage of generating electricity using nuclear power in the UK. **[2 marks]**

Advantage: _____

_____

Disadvantage: _____

_____

1 0 Look at **Figure 13**, a pie chart showing the average background radiation in the UK.

Figure 13

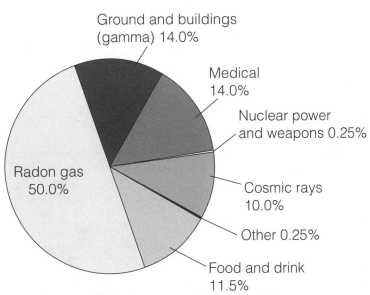

Ground and buildings (gamma) 14.0%

Medical 14.0%

Nuclear power and weapons 0.25%

Cosmic rays 10.0%

Other 0.25%

Food and drink 11.5%

Radon gas 50.0%

1 0 . 1 The actual exposure for each person in the UK may be slightly different than the average.

Suggest **two** reasons why there is a difference. **[2 marks]**

_____

_____

_____

1 0 . 2 Describe **two** precautions workers in the nuclear industry take to reduce their exposure to radiation. **[2 marks]**

_____

_____

1 0 . 3 An average person in the UK receives a dose of 3000 µSv of radiation per year.

How much of an average person's dose comes from medical treatments?
Show all your working.

[2 marks]

_____

_____

1 0 . 4 Gamma radiation can be used to treat cancer tumours.

Explain why gamma radiation can be used to treat cancer. Describe the risks and how the risks are controlled.

[6 marks]

_____

_____

_____

_____

_____

_____

_____

_____

_____

_____

1 1 As shown in **Figure 14**, air is being pumped into a bicycle tyre.

Figure 14

1 1 . 1 The tyre gets harder as more air is pumped into it. Explain how the air inside the tyre produces a pressure. **[2 marks]**

_____

_____

1 1 . 2 Outline why the pressure increases as more air is pumped in. **[1 mark]**

_____

_____

1 1 . 3 A bicycle pump contains 20 cm³ of air at a pressure of 100 kPa. The air is pumped in a single stroke through the valve into the tyre of volume 100 cm³, which contains air at the same pressure.

Calculate the pressure of the air in the tyre after the stroke. **[3 marks]**

_____

_____

END OF QUESTIONS

GCSE
PHYSICS
Higher Tier Paper 2H

Time allowed: 1 hour 45 minutes

You may use:

- a ruler
- a calculator
- a protractor
- the Physics Equation sheet.

Instructions

- Answer all questions in the spaces provided.
- Do all rough work in this book. Cross through any work you do not want to be marked.

Information

- There are 100 marks available on this paper.
- The marks for questions are shown in brackets.
- You are expected to use a calculator where appropriate.
- You are reminded of the need for good English and clear presentation in your answers.
- When answering questions 10.5 and 13.1 you need to make sure that your answer:
  - is clear, logical, sensibly structured
  - fully meets the requirements of the question
  - shows that each separate point or step supports the overall answer.

Advice

- In all calculations, show clearly how you work out your answer.

Name: _____

| 0 | 1 | Look at **Figure 1**, which shows a velocity–time graph of a car travelling on a road.

Figure 1

| 0 | 1 |.| 1 | What is the velocity of the car after two seconds? [1 mark]

_____

| 0 | 1 |.| 2 | Calculate the acceleration of the car between points **A** and **B**.
Show all your working and include the unit in your answer. [3 marks]

_____

_____

_____

_____

| 0 | 1 |.| 3 | Calculate the distance travelled between 0 and 6 seconds. Show all your working. [3 marks]

_____

_____

_____

| 0 | 1 |.| 4 | Describe the motion of the car between points **C** and **D**. [2 marks]

_____

_____

This question is about waves.

Look at **Figure 2**, which shows a wave.

Figure 2

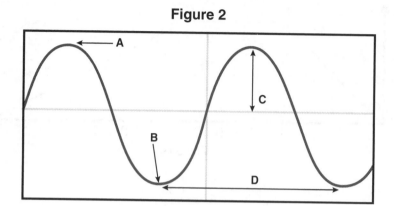

Which letter represents the amplitude of the wave?

Tick (✓) **one** box. **[1 mark]**

A ☐

B ☐

C ☐

D ☐

| 0 | 2 |.| 2 | Microwaves can be used to cook food in a microwave oven, shown in **Figure 3**. Microwaves are part of the electromagnetic spectrum.

Figure 3

Which other part of the electromagnetic spectrum is commonly used to cook food? **[1 mark]**

_____

| 0 | 2 |.| 3 | The microwaves used in ovens have a wavelength of 0.12 m.

The speed of electromagnetic waves is 3×10^8 m/s.

Calculate the frequency of the microwaves used in ovens. Show all your working and include the unit.

[3 marks]

_____

_____

_____

0 3 This question is about space physics.

0 3 . 1 What type of body will a star about the size of the Sun form at the end of its life?
Tick (✓) **one** box.

[1 mark]

Black dwarf ☐

Black hole ☐

Neutron star ☐

Red super giant ☐

0 3 . 2 As shown in **Figure 4**, communication satellites have a circular orbit around Earth.

Figure 4

Which one of the following statements about the motion of a communication satellite is correct?
Tick (✓) **one** box.

[1 mark]

The satellite has both constant speed and constant velocity. ☐

The satellite has both changing speed and changing velocity. ☐

The satellite has constant speed and changing velocity. ☐

The satellite has changing speed and constant velocity. ☐

0 3 . 3 Describe how dust and gas in space becomes a star.

[3 marks]

_____

_____

_____

_____

0 4 David and Gemma are investigating the motion of a toy car. David says that the car will go down the ramp at constant velocity. Gemma disagrees. She thinks the car will gradually go faster.

They design the experiment shown in **Figure 5** to settle the argument. Light gates are attached to a data logger that records the time the car passes through.

Figure 5

0 4 . 1 Explain why David and Gemma must use three light gates to time the car. **[1 mark]**

_____

_____

0 4 . 2 Describe how they can use the times to decide who is correct. **[2 marks]**

_____

_____

_____

0 4 . 3 **Table 1** shows their results.

Table 1

	Run 1	Run 2	Run 3	Run 4
Time at A (s)	0	0	0	0
Time at B (s)	0.141	0.229	0.152	0.139
Time at C (s)	0.249	0.342	0.270	0.251

Identify the anomalous result.
Tick (✓) **one** box. **[1 mark]**

Run 1 ☐

Run 2 ☐

Run 3 ☐

Run 4 ☐

| 0 | 4 | . | 4 | The distance between light gate A and light gate C is 1.50 m.

Ignoring the anomalous result, calculate the overall mean speed of the car from the other runs, in m/s. Show all your working and give your answer to the appropriate number of significant figures.

[3 marks]

_____

_____

_____

_____

_____ m/s

| 0 | 5 | This question is about forces.

| 0 | 5 | . | 1 | **Figure 6** shows an astronaut doing a spacewalk. He can move about using small jets of air blown in directions A, B, C and D. He is stationary.

Figure 6

Which two jets should the astronaut use to move in the direction of the arrow shown?
Tick (✓) **one** box.

[1 mark]

A and B ☐

A and D ☐

B and C ☐

C and D ☐

0 5 . 2 **Figure 7** shows a skydiver.

Figure 7

X

Y

X and Y are forces acting on the skydiver as she falls. Describe what happens to the size of force X as she accelerates.

[1 mark]

_____

0 5 . 3 The skydiver in **Figure 7** has a weight of 550 N.

What will be the value of force X when she stops accelerating and falls at terminal velocity? Explain your answer.

[2 marks]

_____

_____

0 5 . 4 **Figure 8** shows the velocity of the skydiver as she descends through the air.

Figure 8

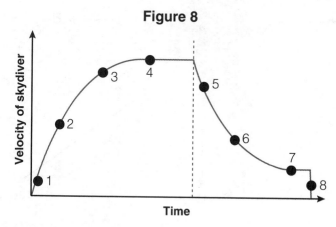

Between which two points does the skydiver open her parachute?
Tick (✓) **one** box.

[1 mark]

4 and 5 ☐

5 and 6 ☐

6 and 7 ☐

7 and 8 ☐

0 5 . 5 Explain why the skydiver has a lower terminal velocity when the parachute is open. **[4 marks]**

_____

_____

_____

_____

0 6 This question is about magnets and their magnetic field.

0 6 . 1 **Figure 9** illustrates an experiment to show a magnetic field around a bar magnet using plotting compasses.

Figure 9

Which direction will the arrow point in the top plotting compass?
Tick (✓) **one** box. **[1 mark]**

0 6 . 2 Look at **Figure 10**.

Figure 10

Describe what happens to the plotting compass arrows when the current is switched on.

[2 marks]

_____

_____

0 6 . 3 Raj is trying to make an electromagnet that will pick up as many paperclips as possible. As shown in **Figure 11**, he adds a soft iron core to the coil.

Figure 11

What **two** other changes could he make to increase the strength of the electromagnet?

[2 marks]

_____

_____

0 6 . 4 As shown in **Figure 12**, a wire is placed in a magnetic field and the current is switched on.

Figure 12

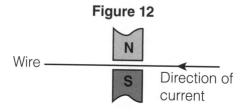

In what direction will the wire move?
Tick (✓) **one** box.

[1 mark]

Down into the page, away from you ☐

Towards the north pole of the magnet ☐

Towards the south pole of the magnet ☐

Up from the page, towards you ☐

0 6 . 5 Explain why the wire only moves once the current is on.

[2 marks]

_____

_____

_____

0 7 **Figure 13** is a simple diagram of the structure of a digital camera.

Figure 13

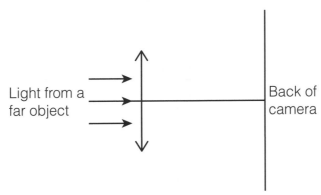

Light from a far object

Back of camera

0 7 . 1 Complete **Figure 13** to show how an image from a far object is formed on the back of the camera. **[2 marks]**

0 7 . 2 Isaac is using the camera to photograph a small flower close up but the image is out of focus. What must happen to the lens to focus the image? **[1 mark]**

_____

_____

0 7 . 3 The flower has a height of 3 mm but it focuses on the back of the camera with a height of 16.5 mm.

Use the formula below to calculate the image magnification. Show all your working. **[2 marks]**

$$\text{magnification} = \frac{\text{image height}}{\text{object height}}$$

_____

_____

_____

0 7 . 4 When a white light is shone on the flower it appears to be a red colour. When a blue light is shone on the flower it appears to be black. Explain these observations. **[4 marks]**

_____

_____

_____

_____

_____

0 8 Navjot and Shaleen are investigating the forces involved in floating and sinking.
Figure 14 shows their experiment.

Figure 14

Spring balance

Rock

Water

0 8 . 1 Describe what happens to the reading on the spring balance as Navjot and Shaleen slowly lower the rock into the water until it is fully submerged. **[2 marks]**

_____

_____

0 8 . 2 Navjot and Shaleen want to produce a graph to show how the force changes. Describe how they can improve their method to produce data that can be plotted on a line graph. **[2 marks]**

_____

_____

_____

0 8 . 3 Label the axes on **Figure 15** to show how Navjot and Shaleen could plot their results. **[1 mark]**

Figure 15

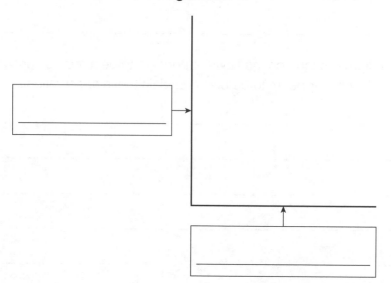

0 8 . 4 Explain why, theoretically, a ship would rise as it travelled from fresh water into seawater.

[3 marks]

_____

_____

_____

_____

0 8 . 5 A diver uses echo sounding from his boat to measure the depth of water, as shown in **Figure 16**.

Figure 16

The pulse of sound takes 0.0270 s to be reflected back to be detected on the boat. If sound travels at a speed of 1500 m/s in water, what is the depth of the water in metres under the boat? Show all your working.

[3 marks]

_____

_____

_____

_____

0 8 . 6 Josh wears a pressure gauge on his wrist. He notices that when he dives 10 m under the water, the pressure around him doubles. When he climbs 10 m to the top of the boat the pressure hardly changes at all.

Explain these observations.

[2 marks]

> pressure = height of column × density of fluid × gravitational field strength

_____

_____

_____

09 | **Figure 17** shows a transformer.

Figure 17

The primary coil has 50 turns and a potential difference of 20 V ac.

09.1 Use the formula $\frac{V_p}{V_s} = \frac{n_p}{n_s}$ to calculate the number of turns needed on the secondary coil to give an output potential difference of 80 V. Show all your working. **[2 marks]**

_____

_____

_____

09.2 What type of transformer converts the potential difference from 20 V to 80 V? **[1 mark]**

_____

09.3 How does this type of transformer alter the current flowing in the secondary circuit? **[1 mark]**

_____

09.4 Explain why a transformer will not operate if the primary coil is connected to a dc supply. **[2 marks]**

_____

_____

_____

_____

10 This question is about the physics of cars and driving.

10.1 Which of the following is a vector quantity?
Tick (✓) **one** box. **[1 mark]**

Distance ☐

Mass ☐

Speed ☐

Velocity ☐

1 0 . 2 **Figure 18** shows a car in a crash test. The car has a mass of 1200 kg.

Figure 18

The car travels at a velocity of 20 m/s. Calculate the total momentum of the car.
Show all your working. **[2 marks]**

_____

_____

_____

1 0 . 3 When the car is crashed into a wall its momentum becomes zero in 0.50 seconds.
What is the size of the force that the car exerts on the wall? **[2 marks]**

$$\text{force} = \frac{\text{change in momentum}}{\text{time}}$$

_____

_____

_____

1 0 . 4 A car driver's awareness of stopping distances is an important part of driving safely. Stopping distance can be affected by tiredness. Why is tiredness not a very good variable for a scientific experiment? **[1 mark]**

_____

| 1 | 0 |.| 5 | The thinking distance and the braking distance can be affected by different factors. Explain how speed, alcohol and road conditions can affect driving safety. **[6 marks]**

_____

_____

_____

_____

_____

_____

_____

_____

_____

| 1 | 1 | The Big Bang theory is often used to explain creation of the universe.

| 1 | 1 |.| 1 | Red-shift is part of the evidence that scientists use to support the Big Bang theory.

Explain what is meant by the term red-shift. **[2 marks]**

_____

_____

| 1 | 1 |.| 2 | Describe and explain how light from galaxies close to us differs from light from very distant galaxies. **[3 marks]**

_____

_____

_____

| 1 | 1 |.| 3 | The Big Bang theory is widely accepted but it may be changed by scientists in the future. Explain why it may change. **[1 mark]**

_____

_____

| 1 | 2 | This question is about force.

| 1 | 2 |.| 1 | As **Figure 19** shows, Adam is trying to turn a nut with a spanner to release some equipment, but it is stuck.

Figure 19

Nut

Spanner

Outline **two** ways Adam could increase the turning effect (moment) on the nut. **[2 marks]**

_____

_____

1 2 . 2 When the forcemeter A was used on its own on the spanner to loosen a nut it read 200N.
Forcemeter B was then used on its own to loosen the nut and it read 300 N.

[3 marks]

Calculate distance X.

_____

_____

_____

1 3 This question is about the application of electromagnetic waves.

1 3 . 1 X rays and ultrasound are both electromagnetic waves.

Explain how and why ultrasound is used to observe an unborn foetus, whereas X-rays aren't.

[6 marks]

_____

_____

_____

_____

_____

_____

_____

_____

END OF QUESTIONS

Notes

Notes

Physics Equations

force = mass × acceleration

kinetic energy = 0.5 × mass × (speed)^2

momentum = mass × velocity

work done = force × distance (along the line of action of the force)

$$\text{power} = \frac{\text{work done}}{\text{time}}$$

$$\text{efficiency} = \frac{\text{output energy transfer}}{\text{input energy transfer}}$$

gravity force = mass × gravity constant (*g*)

potential energy = mass × height × gravitational constant (*g*) in a gravitational field

force exerted by a spring = extension × spring constant

moment of a force = force × distance (normal to direction of the force)

distance travelled = speed × time

$$\text{acceleration} = \frac{\text{change in velocity}}{\text{time}}$$

wave speed = frequency × wavelength

charge flow = current × time

potential difference = current × resistance

power = potential difference × current = (current)^2 × resistance

energy transferred = power × time = charge flow × potential difference

Physics Equations

$$density = \frac{mass}{volume}$$

$$pressure = \frac{force \; normal \; to \; a \; surface}{area \; of \; that \; surface}$$

(final velocity)^2 − (initial velocity)^2 = 2 × acceleration × distance

change in thermal energy = m × specific heat capacity × change in temperature

thermal energy for a change of state = m × specific latent heat

energy transferred in stretching = 0.5 × spring constant × (extension)^2

potential difference across primary coil
× current in primary coil $=$ potential difference across secondary coil
× current in secondary coil

pressure × volume = constant (for a given mass of gas and at a constant temperature) [for gases]

 force on a conductor (at right angles to a magnetic field) carrying a current = magnetic flux density × current × length

$$\frac{potential \; difference \; across \; primary \; coil}{potential \; difference \; across \; secondary \; coil} = \frac{number \; of \; turns \; in \; primary \; coil}{number \; of \; turns \; in \; secondary \; coil}$$

pressure due to a column of liquid = height of column × density of liquid × g

The Periodic Table

Key

Metals

Non-metals

Relative atomic mass →	1
Atomic symbol →	**H**
Name →	hydrogen
Atomic number →	1

0 or 8

1	2												3	4	5	6	7	4 **He** helium 2
7 **Li** lithium 3	9 **Be** beryllium 4												11 **B** boron 5	12 **C** carbon 6	14 **N** nitrogen 7	16 **O** oxygen 8	19 **F** fluorine 9	20 **Ne** neon 10
23 **Na** sodium 11	24 **Mg** magnesium 12												27 **Al** aluminium 13	28 **Si** silicon 14	31 **P** phosphorus 15	32 **S** sulfur 16	35.5 **Cl** chlorine 17	40 **Ar** argon 18
39 **K** potassium 19	40 **Ca** calcium 20	45 **Sc** scandium 21	48 **Ti** titanium 22	51 **V** vanadium 23	52 **Cr** chromium 24	55 **Mn** manganese 25	56 **Fe** iron 26	59 **Co** cobalt 27	59 **Ni** nickel 28	63.5 **Cu** copper 29	65 **Zn** zinc 30	70 **Ga** gallium 31	73 **Ge** germanium 32	75 **As** arsenic 33	79 **Se** selenium 34	80 **Br** bromine 35	84 **Kr** krypton 36
85 **Rb** rubidium 37	88 **Sr** strontium 38	89 **Y** yttrium 39	91 **Zr** zirconium 40	93 **Nb** niobium 41	96 **Mo** molybdenum 42	[98] **Tc** technetium 43	101 **Ru** ruthenium 44	103 **Rh** rhodium 45	106 **Pd** palladium 46	108 **Ag** silver 47	112 **Cd** cadmium 48	115 **In** indium 49	119 **Sn** tin 50	122 **Sb** antimony 51	128 **Te** tellurium 52	127 **I** iodine 53	131 **Xe** xenon 54
133 **Cs** caesium 55	137 **Ba** barium 56	139 **La*** lanthanum 57	178 **Hf** hafnium 72	181 **Ta** tantalum 73	184 **W** tungsten 74	186 **Re** rhenium 75	190 **Os** osmium 76	192 **Ir** iridium 77	195 **Pt** platinum 78	197 **Au** gold 79	201 **Hg** mercury 80	204 **Tl** thallium 81	207 **Pb** lead 82	209 **Bi** bismuth 83	[209] **Po** polonium 84	[210] **At** astatine 85	[222] **Rn** radon 86
[223] **Fr** francium 87	[226] **Ra** radium 88	[227] **Ac*** actinium 89	[261] **Rf** rutherfordium 104	[262] **Db** dubnium 105	[266] **Sg** seaborgium 106	[264] **Bh** bohrium 107	[277] **Hs** hassium 108	[268] **Mt** meitnerium 109	[271] **Ds** darmstadtium 110	[272] **Rg** roentgenium 111							

Elements with atomic numbers 112–116 have been reported but not fully authenticated

*The lanthanoids (atomic numbers 58–71) and the actinoids (atomic numbers 90–103) have been omitted.

The relative atomic masses of copper and chlorine have not been rounded to the nearest whole number.